FOUNDATIONS OF MODERN ECONOMICS SERIES

Otto Eckstein, *Editor*

PUBLISHED

IN PRESS

FOUNDATIONS OF MODERN ECONOMICS SERIES

CHARLES L. SCHULTZE *Senior Fellow,*
*The Brookings Institution*
*Professor of Economics, University of Maryland*

# National Income
# Analysis

**THIRD EDITION**

**PRENTICE-HALL, INC.** *Englewood Cliffs, New Jersey*

13–609420–1

Library of Congress Catalog Number 72–140763

PRENTICE-HALL FOUNDATIONS
OF MODERN ECONOMICS SERIES

Otto Eckstein, *Editor*

Current printing (last digit):
10   9   8   7   6   5   4   3   2   1

PRENTICE-HALL INTERNATIONAL INC., *London*
PRENTICE-HALL OF AUSTRALIA, PTY., LTD., *Sydney*
PRENTICE-HALL OF CANADA, LTD., *Toronto*
PRENTICE-HALL OF INDIA PVT. LIMITED, *New Delhi*
PRENTICE-HALL OF JAPAN, INC., *Tokyo*

# Foundations

# of Modern Economics Series

Economics has grown so rapidly in recent years, it has increased so much in scope and depth, and the new dominance of the empirical approach has so transformed its character, that no one book can do it justice today. To fill this need, the Foundations of Modern Economics Series was conceived. The Series, brief books written by leading specialists, reflects the structure, content, and key scientific and policy issues of each field. Used in combination, the Series provides the material for the basic one-year college course. The analytical core of economics is presented in *Prices and Markets* and *National Income Analysis,* which are basic to the various fields of application. *The Price System* is a more sophisticated alternative introduction to microeconomics. Two books in the Series, *Evolution of Modern Economics* and *Economic Development: Past and Present*, can be read without prerequisite and can serve as an introduction to the subject.

For the third editions, the books have been thoroughly revised and updated. Topics that have come into the forefront of attention have been added or expanded. To preserve the virtues of brevity, older material has been weeded out. A new book has been added to the Series, *Managerial Economics*, by Farrar and Meyer, designed to show more fully how economic reasoning can be applied to decisions in the business firm.

The Foundations approach enables an instructor to devise his own course curriculum rather than to follow the format of the traditional textbook. Once analytical principles have been mastered, many sequences of topics can be arranged and specific areas can be explored at length. An instructor not interested in a complete survey course can omit some books and concentrate on a detailed study of a few fields. One-semester courses stressing either macro- or micro-economics can be readily devised. The Instructors Guide to the Series indicates the variety of ways the books in the Series can be used.

This Series is an experiment in teaching. The continued positive response has encouraged us to continue to develop this new approach. The thoughtful reaction and classroom reports from teachers have helped us once more in preparing the third editions. The Series is used both as a substitute for the basic textbook and as supplementary reading in elementary and intermediate courses.

The books do not offer settled conclusions. They introduce the central problems of each field and indicate how economic analysis enables the reader to think more intelligently about them, in order to make him a more thoughtful citizen and to encourage him to pursue the subject further.

Otto Eckstein, *Editor*

# Contents

vii

# National Income Analysis

## CHAPTER ONE

Economics has been described as a study of man in his ordinary business of making a living. As such it would seem to be a most prosaic and unromantic discipline. Yet because of differences in economic philosophy, men have been willing to spill one another's blood at revolutionary barricades, economic doctrines have been raised to the status of theologies, and conflicting economic ambitions have touched off major wars. Much of what we call Western civilization would be impossible had not economic growth in the last 500 years eased the burden of producing our daily needs. Man may indeed still earn his daily bread by the "sweat of his brow," but the nature of society will depend, in a very important way, on how much "bread" he can obtain by his efforts and on the way in which society organizes those efforts.

## WHAT IS ECONOMICS?

The term "economics" derives from two Greek words, *oikou* and *nomos*, meaning the rule or law of the household. It originally dealt with the way in which the prudent householder might make the most efficient use of his limited income. It calls to mind a picture of the good Athenian housewife frugally budgeting her slender resources to provide the best possible food, clothing, and shelter for her family.

The concept of the efficient use of resources on the part of the household members was later carried over to society as a whole. For this broader setting, economics analyzes how a *society* utilizes its scarce resources of manpower, raw materials, and capital to satisfy the material

1

wants of its members, and how the results of this activity are distributed among those members. What, for example, determines how much steel and manpower are devoted to the production of automobiles and how much to the output of tin cans or refrigerators? How is it determined that a fully employed steel worker earns, on the average, $7,000 per year, and the president of a large corporation $350,000? More than seeking to understand how a given society actually allocates its scarce resources among different uses, economics also seeks to formulate criteria that would achieve the best possible allocation of resources.

This definition of economics, couched principally in terms of using scarce resources to satisfy human wants, is correct enough, as far as it goes. But it is incomplete. It evokes the picture of a society with *fixed* resources, skills, and productive capacity deciding what specific kinds of goods it ought to produce and how they ought to be distributed. The major role of economics seems to be the study of how best to utilize a *fixed and fully employed* productive potential. Yet two of the most important concerns of modern economics are not fully covered by this concept.

On the one hand, the productive capacity of modern economies, far from remaining stable, has grown tremendously. Population and the labor force have increased; new sources of raw materials have been discovered; and an ever-growing volume of plant and equipment has been made available on farms and in factories and mines. Not only has the *quantity* of available productive resources increased, but their *quality* has also been greatly improved. Education and newly acquired skills have raised the productivity of the labor force; completely new kinds of natural resources—petroleum and atomic energy, for example—have appeared; and the efficiency of industrial machinery and equipment has been constantly upgraded. *Economic growth* has been a characteristic of modern industrial economies, and explaining the factors that lead to growth is an important part of economics. On the other hand, the resulting growth in production and income has not been smooth. It has frequently been interrupted by periods in which output not only failed to grow but actually declined sharply. During such periods, while pressing human wants go unsatisfied, men and factories stand idle, lacking sufficient markets for what they produce. It is not enough to have a large and growing productive potential; that potential must be fully employed in the production of goods and services if we are to avoid widespread economic distress.

In outline form we can summarize the major concerns of economics in the following way:

1. Problems of production and distribution:
   - *what* specific goods and services are produced in what quantities?
   - *how* are they produced?
   - *who* gets the results?

2. Problems of economic growth:
   - how can a society increase its over-all *capacity* to produce goods and services?

*major concerns of economics*

3. Problems of economic stability:
   - what causes society's over-all *demand* for goods and services sometimes to fall below the economy's capacity to produce (leading to unemployment) and sometimes to run ahead of capacity (leading to inflation)?

Economics, therefore, does not concern itself only with how a nation allocates to various uses a constant quantity and quality of productive resources— the first problem listed above. It also deals with the process by which the productive capacity of these resources is increased and with the factors that have led to sharp fluctuations in the rate of utilization of resources. These last two aspects of economic analysis, growth and stability, are the major subjects of this book.

*\ main aspects / of Economic*

## ECONOMIC GROWTH

In 1969 the value of all goods and services produced in the United States amounted to some $932 billion. Guns and butter, electricity and haircuts, television sets and machine tools, symphony concerts and children's toys—all these and a host of other goods and services were part of the total. Dividing $932 billion by the 1969 population of 203 million, we arrive at a per-capita figure of about $4,600. Hardly more than 100 years ago—and a hundred years is not really so long in the sweep of human history—the average per-capita value of national output was about $650, one-seventh as large. In the ten decades since the Civil War, per-capita production in the United States has grown by an average of 18 per cent per decade.[1]

Accompanying this rise in the national output and income has been an equally impressive rise in the quality of goods and services we enjoy. For all his wealth, Louis XIV had to shiver in the draughty rooms of Versailles for lack of central heating. If he wanted to journey from Paris to Marseilles—a distance of 400 miles—he had to suffer through a bumpy, uncomfortable 10-day trip in a horse-drawn coach. Today, most families have central heating and an automobile.

The phenomenal growth in the quality and quantity of goods and services produced in the Western world has been widely distributed. There are, indeed, many American and Western European families whose incomes, even in times of prosperity, fail to provide a minimum standard of decent living. But mass starvation in the Western world is a thing of the past. As the national incomes of Western nations have risen, extensive social-security and social-welfare programs have been created, assisting those with inadequate incomes. Indeed, one of the chief problems of the very lowest income groups is not so much their failure to find enough to eat, but the contrast between their own poverty and the living standards of the vast majority. In general, it is fair to say that the fruits of

[1]Both figures, 1969 and 1865, are expressed in dollars of constant purchasing power, so that we may see the increase in the real value of output, undistorted by mere price increases.

economic progress in the Western world have been widely shared, and not confined to any select minority.

The reward of economic growth is a rise in living standards. But that same growth also has its costs. To wrest from nature an increasing abundance of material goods, new and better ways of combining natural resources, human labor, and human ingenuity must be introduced. Old techniques of production must give way to new, old goods to new goods, and old methods of organization to new ones. Incessant change is the hallmark of rising per-capita incomes. But change requires adaptation, and adaptation is often painful. If over-all economic prosperity is maintained, new jobs are created to replace the ones destroyed. But this may be cold comfort for the older worker and the "one-industry" town, for whom technological progress may mean years of unemployment and economic decay. The new jobs may be far distant from the homes of those displaced, or may require skills the displaced do not possess. Indeed, the fortunes of entire communities can be destroyed by technological advance. As electric power displaced water power, hundreds of textile mills, based on the water power of the rapid New England streams, were forced to close. Today one can drive through entire towns, virtually abandoned, their mills silent and their homes deserted. The coming of petroleum and natural gas, of diesel-powered trains and the modern trucking industry, have cut deeply into the market for coal. The thousands of unemployed in the mining towns of eastern Kentucky, West Virginia, and Pennsylvania are grim reminders of the cost of economic progress.

## ECONOMIC INSTABILITY

Besides the *specific, localized* pockets of unemployment left in the wake of economic progress, the economies of the Western world have been subject to the period occurrence of *mass* unemployment. During the last century the course of economic growth has all too frequently been interrupted by depressions. In the United States the years 1872, 1882, 1893, 1907, 1920, and 1929 each marked the beginning of a major downturn in production and employment. During these depressions output and income fell sharply, factories stood idle for lack of markets, and unemployed workers went without income in a land of potential plenty. There was not a year between 1930 and 1939, for example, in which the number of workers without a job was less than 1 out of 6. There was not a year in which steel mills operated at more than 73 per cent of their capacity. In the words of President Franklin Roosevelt, "one-third of the nation [was] ill-clothed, ill-fed, and ill-housed," and this in a country with prodigious capacity to turn out goods and services of every description.

In between the major depressions, there have also occurred numerous smaller declines. Since World War II, for example, there have been four "reces-

sions," as it is popular to call such <u>moderate downturns</u>. But, significantly, there recessions are moderate downturns.
have been no repetitions of the severe prewar depressions.

In terms of the numbers of people affected and the magnitude of income
and production lost, economic depression has been a far more serious problem
than the specific and localized unemployment we discussed in the last section.
The latter, painful as it is to those concerned, is a matter of particular individuals,
communities, or industries. <u>This localized unemployment is called *structural* unemployment,</u> since it is occasioned by the difficulties of individuals and com- structural un-n
munities in adjusting to changes in economic structure. <u>*General,* or *mass,* unem-</u> general un-n
<u>ployment,</u> on the other hand, <u>reflects a widespread decline of economic activity,</u>
more severe in some industries and communities than in others, but reaching,
nevertheless, into almost every community and every industry.[2]

In many ways the occurrence of general unemployment is a cruel paradox.
If the economic misery that accompanies depression resulted from the *inability* of
society to produce enough food, shelter, and clothing to meet the needs of its
members, this would be tragic, but unavoidable. In many parts of the world today
productive capacity is barely sufficient to provide people with a minimum of
subsistence. When natural forces such as floods or unfavorable weather ruin a
harvest, even this minimum is threatened; the very real terror of famine and mass
starvation has not yet been banished from our planet. Modern warfare can also
leave a nation with its industry shattered and its standard of living drastically
reduced. Unemployment is high because the factories and transportation facilities
that provide employment have been destroyed. Again tragic—but understand-
able. <u>The chief feature of economic depressions, however, is that they occur in</u>
<u>nations that *have the capacity* to turn out an abundance of goods and services.</u>
People do without clothing while textile factories and textile workers are idle for
want of a market! The building of new houses falls off, not because building materials or labor is unavailable, but because homes cannot be sold. Yet, at the same
time there are millions of families who live in substandard housing. The factories,
the skills, the raw materials, the willingness to work and to produce are all there
—but there is no production.

There are other times when the economy races ahead under inflationary
conditions. The demand for goods and services by consumers, business investors,
and government exceeds the nation's capacity to produce. Unemployment falls
to very low levels; workers are in short supply as business firms anxiously seek
to expand production. Unions seek and gain very large wage increases. Business
firms are able to pass these cost increases on, and then some, to booming markets.
During World War II and in its immediate aftermath, during the Korean war,
again briefly in the mid-1950s, and finally during the Vietnam war, such condi-

---

[2]*General* unemployment is often called "Keynesian" unemployment by economists. The name
refers to John Maynard Keynes, the famous English economist, whose 1936 book, *The General Theory
of Employment, Interest and Money,* is the basis for most modern analyses of general unemployment.

tions prevailed in varying degrees. The nation as a whole was seeking to buy more than its productive capacity could turn out. Inflation resulted.

We must distinguish, therefore, between what a nation *can* produce when it is fully utilizing its productive resources and what it actually does produce. What it can produce we shall call its *potential output;* what it does produce we call its *actual output*. In general, the problem of economic growth deals with the factors that increase a nation's potential output—its productive capacity. The problem of economic instability involves the fact that actual output often falls below potential output, because purchases by businessmen and consumers are too low to provide a market for potential output. It is also possible for a nation to attempt to purchase more goods and services than it is capable of producing— to attempt to push its actual output well beyond its potential. In this case, economic instability takes the form of inflation, as demand exceeds supply and prices are driven upward.

The distinction between actual and potential output is crucial. When low production and depressed living standards result because actual output is below potential output, the major problem is one of insufficient markets; men and factories are idle because the demand for their output is not high enough to keep them fully employed. Hence an improvement in living standards and a return to prosperity can be achieved only if markets are expanded through a rise in purchases of goods and services. Idle plants and unemployed workers are available to turn out an increased volume of output. But in an economy whose actual output is already equal to its potential, whose workers and factories are fully employed, further gains in output and consequently in living standards can occur only if the potential expands. The problems of economic growth (expansion of potential output) and economic stability (keeping actual output up to potential) will occupy us for the remaining chapters.

## POSITIVE AND NORMATIVE ECONOMICS

About each of the three basic problems with which economics deals we can ask two different kinds of questions. First, in a particular society—the United States, France, the Soviet Union—how does the economy actually behave? In the United States, Western Europe, and most of the countries outside of the Soviet and Chinese blocs, for example, production and distribution primarily depend upon the independent decisions of thousands of business firms and millions of consumers. The economy, considered as a whole, is incredibly complex and interrelated.

How is it that the millions of individual decisions result not in economic chaos but, under most circumstances, in a relatively abundant outpouring of goods and services? What factors actually determine the rate of economic growth in the United States? What forces lead to inflation and recessions? *Positive economics* deals with these kinds of questions. It looks at reality and seeks to find patterns and relationships that help to explain why things happen the way they do. If consumer income rises by 10 per cent, what is likely to happen to consumer expenditures? If businessmen increase their investment in plant and equipment, what will be the effect on the rate of economic growth? If a competitive industry gradually becomes monopolized, with one or a few firms securing the bulk of the business, what will be the likely effect on production, prices, and jobs in that industry?

Whereas positive economics deals with the world as it is, *normative economics* deals with the world as it "should" be. Starting principally with the ethical assumption that the economy ought to serve the wants of the individual members of society, normative economics investigates the problem of how an economy can best serve those wants. In an economy with a substantial free enterprise component, for example, normative economics tells us that competition among business firms normally produces "better" results than a cartel or a monopoly—although it says this with certain qualifications and exceptions.[3] Normative economics also seeks to determine what kinds of goods can best be produced under free market conditions and what kinds of goods must be produced on the basis of collective or governmental decisions. Decisions about the production of cosmetics and automobiles and clothespins can effectively be left to the private market. But decisions about the production of national defense and law enforcement and flood control levees must be made collectively. The principal distinguishing characteristic of private goods is that they can be sold for a profit. Public goods cannot be; who would buy one two-hundred-millionth of a strategic nuclear missile force, or one eight-millionth of the New York City Police Department? Such goods must be produced on the basis of collective decisions, in which the individual expresses his views through the political process, not through the market place.

As we noted earlier, normative economics proceeds on the general assumption that an economic system ought to serve the wants of its members. It does not attempt to pass judgment on those wants. Normative economics cannot tell us whether automobiles are better than symphony concerts or pollution control plants more desirable than bubble gum factories. But it does attempt to determine the conditions under which those wants can most effectively be translated into the production of the appropriate goods and services. In common-sense terms, normative economics seeks to tell us how to improve the economic world that positive economics describes. But its criterion of improvement is one that takes the wants of the members of society as supreme—it does not pass ethical judgment on those wants.

---

[3] In the case of such "natural" monopolies as local telephone service, normative economics concludes that monopoly can often give better results than competition but then goes on to deduce the ground rules that a regulatory agency should follow in regulating the monopoly.

## THE CIRCULAR FLOW
## OF ECONOMIC ACTIVITY

Any modern economy consists of a vast interlocking network of relationships. There are few Robinson Crusoes among us. Our jobs, the goods we buy, the safety of the savings we accumulate, all depend on the activities of literally millions of other people, most of whom we do not know and never shall meet. In economic life it is particularly true that "No man is an island unto himself." One of the most important aspects of these relationships, and the one that is the central theme of this book, involves the relations among *total* production, income, and spending. These relations are shown in a simplified form in Fig. 1–1.

Unlike the primitive farmer, who produced everything he needed, modern production is carried on mainly by business firms for sale to others. In order to produce, firms must hire workers and acquire machinery and equipment. Production, therefore, involves the payment of wages and salaries to workers, and interest and dividends to the investors who provide the funds with which the machinery and equipment were purchased. In turn, this income is used by workers and investors to purchase goods and services. Production creates income and income in turn is used to purchase output. Thus each of us has a dual role in the productive process; in our capacity as productive agents—workers or investors—we receive income from business firms; in our capacity as consumers, we pay out income to businesses for the food, clothing, automobiles, and other goods that business firms produce.

The business firm also stands in a dual capacity, paying out income to its workers and investors and selling goods or services to purchasers. All in all, there are four related flows: goods and services flow from firms to purchasers, matched by a return flow of money from purchaser to business firms; the services of individuals, in their role as productive agents, go to firms, and this flow is matched by a return flow of money paid out by firms in the form of wages and other incomes.

Production creates income, income creates spending, and spending calls forth production. There is no beginning point and no ending point in this circular flow. In a primitive economy each man produces most of what he needs; in a sense he is business firm, consumer, and worker all in one. In the modern economy production is so specialized that no man could exist if he received only the results of his own production. Workers in a shoe factory cannot eat shoes, nor can a modern wheat farmer live on wheat alone. From this fact stems the interdependence of modern economic life. The worker in the shoe factory receives a money income for his efforts, and with that income he can purchase the necessities, and perhaps some of the luxuries, he desires. But his livelihood depends on the fact that farmers are buying shoes, just as theirs is dependent on his purchases of food.

In order to produce, a business firm incurs costs. To make production worthwhile, a firm must recover those costs, including the interest and profit it

8

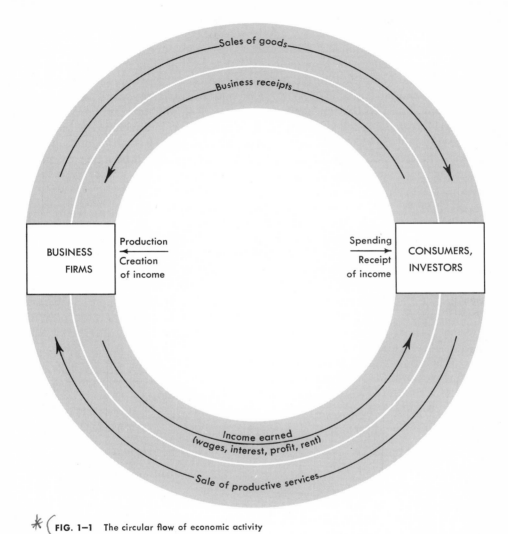

Sales of goods

Business receipts

BUSINESS FIRMS

Production
Creation
of income

Spending
Receipt
of income

CONSUMERS, INVESTORS

Income earned
(wages, interest, profit, rent)

Sale of productive services

**FIG. 1–1**  The circular flow of economic activity

pays to its investors out of the receipts from its customers. What are costs to the firm are incomes to workers and investors. If all that income is spent on purchases of goods and services, then business receipts will cover costs, firms will generally be satisfied to continue the production process, and the circular flow of *production → income → purchases → production* will continue unimpeded.

Abundant production and full employment depend on the continuous and uninterrupted flow of income and purchases. If, therefore, we wish to understand

9

why, in a private-enterprise economy, production has often fallen below what the economy *could* produce, we must seek the explanation in terms of this circular flow.

Suppose, for example, that throughout the economy all the various industries were producing at or near their capacity, and that roughly all the available labor force were employed in the process. In other words, suppose the economy were producing at potential. The value of output would be exactly matched by income, as shown in the left-hand side of Fig. 1–2. But now suppose that the total flow of *spending* fell below the flow of production and income, as indicated by the top half of Fig. 1–2. Unsold stocks of goods would begin to pile up, and business firms would soon be forced to reduce output and production to match

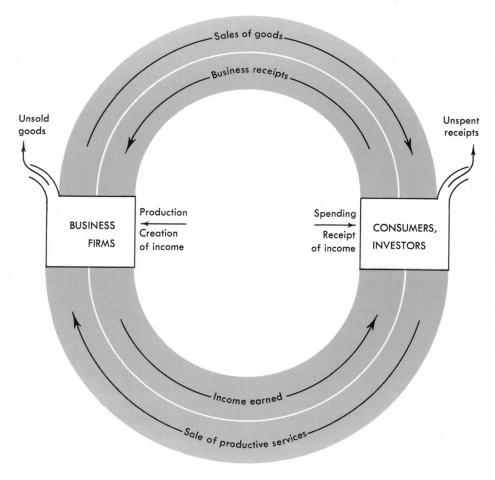

FIG. 1–2  A disruption in the flow of economic activity

the flow of purchases. At some point, sales and production would finally adjust to each other, but *at a lower level*—the economy would be in a depression. On the other hand, if the flow of purchases could be raised to match the flow of production when production was at capacity, then business firms could find a market for their output. The costs incurred in full-capacity production would be matched by receipts from customers, and firms would be willing to produce at that level. Actual output would equal potential output, and prosperity and full employment would return.

*[handwritten margin note: actual & potential output equal means prosperity]*

The illustration is admittedly oversimplified. For example, it does not take into account government taxation and spending—a consideration we add later. But it conveys the major point. The forces that produce fluctuations in the level of business activity and lead to alternating periods of prosperity and depression are to be found in the relation between production, income, and spending.

## TOTAL OUTPUT AND ITS COMPOSITION: MACRO- AND MICRO-ECONOMICS

One of the major principles of economics is that everything depends on everything else. Indeed, as one economist rather ruefully put it, further study indicates that everything depends on everything else in at least two different ways. With tens of thousands of different commodities produced by millions of productive processes and consumed by millions of households, the circular flow of economic activity in a modern society is a closely woven, interlocking mesh, in which each part has some relation, however indirect, with every other part. But the human mind cannot come to grips with such a complicated structure all in one piece. Hence we approach an understanding of economics by isolating particular aspects of the circular flow for separate study. As in all other subjects—history, psychology, physics—we break up the whole field into manageable parts. Understanding each part makes it easier to see how all the parts fit together into a unified whole.

We are concerned in this book with problems of economic growth and stability. We are interested, in other words, in the factors that determine the over-all magnitude of the production and income flows.

Why does the over-all flow of output and income fluctuate, sometimes falling below a nation's capacity to produce, and at other times racing ahead so swiftly as to strain against the limits of available resources? What factors lead to growth in the level of productive capacity, and what are the social and economic costs of growth? The answers to such questions comprise the field of *aggregate economics*. The term "aggregate" is used to emphasize the fact that our interest lies in *total* output and income, rather than in the detailed analysis of their components. Another name for aggregate economics is *macro-economics* (from the Greek word *makros*, meaning "large"). The main tool of this branch of econom-

*[handwritten margin note: aggregate economics equals macro-economics]*

11

ics is _national income analysis,_ the statistical measurement of such aggregate flows as the gross national product; national income, consumption, and investment; and the search for systematic relationships that can explain the changes in these aggregates over time.

The composition of output, the distribution of income, and the workings of the price system are the domain of _micro-economics_ (from the Greek word _mikros,_ meaning "small"). In micro-economics we analyze the price system in order to explain how, in a free-enterprise economy, resources are allocated to the production of _particular_ goods and services and how those goods and services are distributed among the population. In terms of our circular flow diagrams, the task of micro-economics is to explain the composition of the over-all output and income flows (how many millions of automobiles, how many bushels of wheat); the wages of bricklayers versus the wages of accountants; the price of bread versus the price of cigarettes. Price theory is the main tool of micro-economics.

This rough division of labor between macro- and micro-economics, the former analyzing the totals and the latter the composition of the totals, has proven a most useful device. But the divorce cannot be final, for the composition of the parts affects the total, and the size of the total affects the parts.

How efficiently resources are allocated to different uses has a bearing on an economy's over-all level of output. If, for example, we insisted on producing only agricultural products, despite the fact that much of our labor and capital resources were not suited for such work, the total level of production would fall. The over-all level of output and income also depends, in part, on how income is distributed; too great a concentration of income in the hands of a small minority of wealthy people would, in the long run, probably reduce the demand for goods and services and lead to low output and high unemployment. Conversely, complete equality of income—everyone earning precisely as much as his neighbor—might well lead to a reduction in incentives and a slackening of economic growth.

The over-all magnitude of output also affects the composition of output. When total output falls during a depression, the output of durable goods declines more than nondurables, and nondurables decline more than services. Profits fall more than wages, and wages fall more than interest. Although we can and do for purposes of analysis separate macro- from micro-economics, the interrelations between them have to be kept in mind.

The other fields of economics can be related to this macro–micro classification and rely, to various degrees, on the tools developed in national income analysis and price theory. Thus, _labor economics_ is primarily a micro-field dealing with labor markets. _Industrial organization_ analyzes the structures of particular industries and the markets in which they sell their products. _Public finance_ applies both the micro- and the macro-tools to the problems of government, whereas _money and banking_ does the same for the payments and credit system of the modern economy. _International economics_ concentrates on the special features

12

introduced into economic relationships by trade among sovereign nations. *Economic systems* contrasts how the major micro- and macro-problems are solved by socialist and communist economies as compared with our own, and *economic history and development* seeks to apply the relevant tools to explain the progress of the advanced countries and to draw lessons for economies that are still in earlier historical stages.

## TOOLS OF ECONOMIC ANALYSIS

Before we turn to a specific analysis of the problems of economic growth and stability, it will be useful to devote a few pages to a brief introduction to some of the major concepts that underly all aspects of economics.

| Choice |

In the most fundamental sense, economics is an *analysis of the problems of choice*. Even in the wealthiest society human wants still appear virtually insatiable. The United States has the highest per-capita income of any nation in history—and that income increases almost every year, even after we exclude the effect of price increases. Compared to any society in past centuries, and most of those today, we are fabulously rich. Yet there are few among us who could not find plenty of ways to use additional income. And we have become particularly—and perhaps belatedly—aware in recent years that a sizable minority of Americans still live in poverty. Compared to our wants, both individually and as a nation, our means of producing goods and services are limited. We do not possess an infinite supply of productive resources—land, labor, and machinery. The limits with which the United States is faced are high by any historical standard, but limits there are. As a consequence we, and every other society, must choose from a limited set of possibilities the particular goods and services we wish to produce with our productive resources. If we want to increase the production of TV sets, then we must take productive resources away from the production of something else. If we want more guns, we must give up some butter.[4] To devote more resources to education requires that we devote less to something else. People who would have become doctors or lawyers or auto mechanics must be induced to become teachers and school administrators.

Every society must make these choices, literally by the millions; they may be made under different economic systems, but they must be made. Economics deals with the ways in which the choices are arrived at. It seeks both to describe the systems analytically and to suggest ways that choices may be made more

---

[4]The popular slogan "You can't have both guns and butter" is not correct. We can, and always do, have both guns and butter. After all, we do not starve during wars. What is true is that usually we cannot have *more* guns and *more* butter at the same time.

efficiently. If a society could have everything it wanted in the way of material goods and services, if the supply of productive resources were unlimited, there would be no need for choice. But until that day arrives—and neither you nor I will see it—choice is a necessity.

## Opportunity Cost

The necessity for choice leads immediately to the concept of *opportunity costs*, a very important aspect of economics. To General Motors, the cost of an automobile is the sum of the money it must pay out for labor and steel and chrome and machine tools and all the other elements that go into the production of an automobile. But from society's standpoint, the cost of an automobile is the other goods or services that must be sacrificed in order to produce it. The labor and steel and machine tools used to produce an automobile could have been used to turn out TV sets or refrigerators or hospital beds.[5] The monetary costs of production are only symbolic. They are a measure of the value of resources used in the production process—resources that could have been used in producing something else. The real economic cost of producing good $X$ is the opportunity we sacrifice of producing $Y$ or $Z$. Opportunity cost, therefore, represents the foregone production of one good that is required in producing another good.

Opportunity cost is a valuable concept with widespread applications. In many parts of the arid Southwest, for example, water is transported by irrigation canals for use in agriculture. The cost of digging the canals can be computed. But the real economic cost of that water is the industrial production that has to be sacrificed because the water is diverted to agriculture rather than to industrial uses. And, in many cases, the value of the extra agricultural production is far less than the water's opportunity cost—i.e., the foregone industrial production.

In discussing military budgets, many people think that cost is unimportant —that the only relevant consideration in deciding whether to adopt a particular weapon is whether it works well. But if there is a limit to the military budget— set by political or other considerations—then added costs for one weapons system necessarily mean lower procurement of other weapons systems. Hence a particular system should be purchased only if it adds more to the national security than the weapons it necessarily displaces. Or, to say it another way, the contribution to national security of a weapons system should be greater than its opportunity cost; otherwise, the decision to purchase it will reduce the national security, since the weapons such a system displaces (its opportunity cost) are more valuable than it is. It is hard to convince many military people that, even from the strict point of view of providing for the national security, costs are important: they are important not because they are monetary costs, but because they are also opportunity costs; they represent opportunities foregone.

[5]You may object that machine tools used for producing autos are not very useful for turning out hospital beds. True enough. But if the decision had been made in time, those machine tools would have been designed for bed production, not auto production.

### The Production Possibility Curve

At any one point in time, a society has a particular amount of productive resources—land, labor, and capital—which it can employ in the production of goods and services, using the technology of the period. Since resources are in finite supply—i.e., they are not unlimited—there is also a limit to the total volume of production that can be wrung from those resources. But there is an almost infinite number of combinations of particular goods and services that can be produced within that limit. Labor, materials, and machinery can be diverted from the production of furniture to the production of school buildings; pencil output can be reduced and the supply of clothespins increased. There is, in other words, a set of production possibilities that can be achieved; and within the set, various mixtures of different goods and services can be had.

To illustrate, let us imagine an economy with only two kinds of goods and services: TV sets and machine tools. Let us also assume some particular amount of productive resources available to the society, and let us stipulate that these resources are all employed in turning out some combination of TV sets and machine tools. There is no unemployment in our imaginary economy. The hypothetical *production possibilities schedule* of Table 1–1 depicts the combinations available.

**Table 1–1   PRODUCTION POSSIBILITIES SCHEDULE: TV SETS AND MACHINE TOOLS**

| Commodity | Number of Units Per Year (in millions) | | | | | |
|---|---|---|---|---|---|---|
|  | A | B | C | D | E | F |
| Machine tools | 0 | 4 | 7 | 9 | 10 | 11 |
| TV sets | 16 | 14 | 12 | 9 | 5 | 0 |

All the resources of this mythical economy can be used to produce machine tools, in which case we get no TV sets and 11 million machine tools. Conversely, we can pull all the resources out of machine tools output and produce 16 million TV sets per year. In between there exists an infinite number of combinations of TV sets and machine tool production (four of which are shown in the schedule).

The same information can be plotted on a graph (Figure 1–3), which we label the *production possibilities curve*. Each point of the curve represents one possible combination of outputs that can be produced with the resources available. The production possibilities curve (PPC) and its numerical counterpart, the production possibilities schedule (PPS), can be used to illustrate a number of crucial economic concepts.

*Choice.*   As we pointed out earlier, economics fundamentally deals with choice. Every society must have some system of choosing from among the alternative combinations available. It must decide to give up some TV sets to get machine tools or vice versa. It cannot, in the example shown here, produce 14

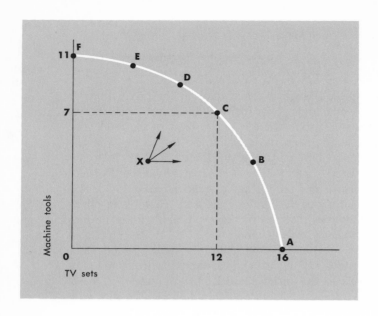

FIG. 1–3 Production possibilities curve, TV sets and machine tools

million TV sets and 9 million machine tools. To get the 14 million TV sets, it must choose to reduce machine tool production to 4 million units.

*Opportunity cost.* The opportunity cost of machine tools is the TV sets we must give up to get them. The opportunity cost of 14 million TV sets is 7 million machine tools—i.e., if we produced *no* TV sets, we could have 11 million machine tools instead of the 4 million that are possible when we turn out 14 million TV sets.

*Marginal cost.* What is the cost of increasing TV production from 9 million units to 12 million units? To do so, we must give up 2 million machine tools. Each additional TV set, at this point, "costs" two thirds of a machine tool. This is the marginal cost of TV sets, namely, the cost of producing an *additional unit*. When TV production is zero, the cost of adding 5 million units is 1 million machine tools—the marginal cost of a TV set in this range is one fifth of a machine tool. When we express marginal costs in terms of what has to be sacrificed in the production of one good in order to increase the production of another good, we can speak of *marginal opportunity costs*.

Marginal cost is an exceedingly important concept in economics. Normally, we are not dealing with "all or nothing" situations. We do not face the choice of completely eliminating TV production and transferring all society's resources to the production of machine tools. Rather, we must choose between increasing (decreasing) machine tool production by some amount and decreasing (increasing) TV production in order to make this possible. Hence it is the cost of adding to machine tool or TV production—the marginal cost of TV sets or machine tools—that is relevant.

16

More to the point, it turns out that making rational choices about which combination of goods to produce involves significantly the concept of marginal costs. Assume that the economy is currently producing at combination C (7 million machine tools, 12 million TV sets). Should production of TV sets be increased and machine tool output lowered? At this point on the PPC, the marginal opportunity cost of a TV set is one and a half machine tools (we give up 3 million machine tools to get 2 million TV sets). If society places a *greater* value on one TV set than it does on one and a half machine tools, then clearly TV production should be increased. We gain more than we lose. If, conversely, the value to society of one TV set is *less* than one and a half machine tools, then production of TV sets should not be increased.

Rational choice from among different alternative uses of productive resources, therefore, depends upon a comparison of marginal opportunity costs with the value that society places on various goods and services. To produce more of one good, we must give up the enjoyment of other goods. If the value of the good whose production is increased is greater than the value of the goods sacrificed, then clearly a switch of resources to the first good is in order. But only by comparing values with marginal opportunity costs can this choice be intelligently made.

In a social system that heavily relies on private enterprise, most "values" are determined in the market place. In the typical socialist economy, values are determined by central planners. But whatever the system for determining values, and whatever mechanism actually prevails for making choices, rational choice should ultimately involve the comparison of social values with marginal opportunity costs.

Micro-economics, in particular, is concerned with the problems of choice. On the one hand, it seeks to spell out the principles for making rational choices in a world where limited productive resources are confronted by unlimited human wants. It also examines the workings of our market economy, to describe analytically how a decentralized market system actually makes choices relating to production and prices; it evaluates the "real world" in the light of the principles of rational choice.

*Increasing marginal cost.* If you calculate the marginal costs of TV sets and machine tools in the hypothetical examples shown in Table 1–1, you will find that they increase as production increases. When TV production rises from zero to 5 million sets, the marginal cost per set is one fifth of a machine tool. This cost increases steadily to the point where, as we reach a production of 14 million TV sets, the marginal cost of producing one more set is two machine tools. The same is true of the marginal cost of machine tools. Although the numbers here are hypothetical, the proposition that marginal costs tend to increase as one moves along the production possibilities curve reflects actual conditions in the economy.

There are several reasons for the general tendency of marginal costs to increase. Resources tend to be specialized in the production of particular goods.

17

As we switch them to other activities, we lose some of the advantages of specialization. Land ideally adapted to the production of rice is less productive for growing corn. If we were to increase the production of corn, at first we would use land highly suitable for that production. But at higher and higher levels of corn production, we would be forced to begin using land less appropriate for corn production. Workers specialized in one occupation may prove to be less efficient when they are shifted to other fields of employment. Moreover, the "ideal" combination of land, labor, and capital is different for different kinds of production. The "mix" of resources we shift out of textile production—which uses much labor and relatively little capital—will not be ideal for petroleum refining, which uses much capital and little labor. For these and other reasons, marginal opportunity costs tend to rise as we shift resources out of one type of production into another.

_Unemployment._    In Fig. 1–3, point $X$ represents a situation of unemployed resources. Point $X$ is _inside_ the production possibilities frontier. In such a situation, the economy is not using all its available labor, land, and capital. By employing its idle resources, the economy could increase production of _both_ TV sets _and_ machine tools. The problems of choice are, in a sense, suspended in a period of substantial unemployment. More of everything can be produced, because resources are idle. Or to put it another way, marginal opportunity costs are zero. The basic choice problem—we can have more of $X$ only if we give up some of $Y$—operates in a full-employment economy,[6] not an economy with large amounts of idle resources.

_Economic growth._    In most modern economies, the production possibilities curve does not stand still. We pointed out earlier that productive capacity tends to rise over time, as the advances of modern technology are incorporated in business plant and equipment and as the spread of education and training produces a more skilled labor force. In Fig. 1–3, the PPC moves out to the right as economic growth occurs. This does not mean that the problems of choice disappear. But the "menu" is richer and more varied.

The PPC shown in Fig. 1–3 also illustrates another point about economic growth. Imagine that TV sets represent all _consumer_ goods in general and machine tools all _investment_ goods; i.e., items of plant and equipment that themselves are used to produce other goods. In this case, a movement "southwest" along the PPC—producing more investment goods and less consumer goods—represents a choice by society to increase its rate of growth. It has decided to divert resources from the production of goods for immediate consumption to the production of goods (plant and equipment) that can be used for increasing future production and consumption. In other words, the rate at which the PPC shifts

---

[6]As we shall see at a later point, "full employment" does not mean a drum-tight economy with all resources 100 per cent employed. Some modest working slack is present in the best-run economy. But for purposes of this discussion, we can ignore refinements of definitions and simply talk about a full-employment economy versus one with a substantial amount of unemployed resources, not worrying about the practical limits to full employment.

out to the right depends, among other things, on what choices are made about the economy's location along the PPC.

## SUPPLY, DEMAND, EQUILIBRIUM

Some of you have already studied micro-economics and are familiar with such basic concepts as the supply curve, the demand curve, and the state of equilibrium. Although many analytical tools were devised particularly for macro-economics, economists bring a common intellectual heritage to all their problems, and some of the essential ideas of micro-economics also find application in the macro-field.

The concept of *equilibrium* is perhaps the most important of these common threads. The concepts of *supply* and *demand* are also found in many areas of economics. They are as fundamental in macro-economics as they are on the micro-side.

Economics is much concerned with markets. In micro-economics we analyze the demand and the supply for specific commodities and how they come together in the market to determine an equilibrium price. In macro-economics we study how the total demand for all goods and services is determined and how large the supply of total production will be. Whereas price brings supply and demand together for a specific commodity, income is the key to equilibrium between aggregate demand and supply.

Before we launch into the analysis of aggregate supply and demand, let us take a quick look at the micro-economic origins of these ideas.[7]

A market contains two groups of participants: buyers and sellers. The buyers want to buy the commodity at as low a price as they can; the sellers are willing to part with it if offered a good enough price. Will sales actually be made? And how many? And at what price?

Figure 1–4a shows the *supply curve* for some hypothetical commodity, *A*. If the price of *A* is low, many sellers will prefer not to sell their supplies of *A*. The producers of *A* will be able to operate only their most efficient plants at a profit. But if the price of *A* rises, more of the potential suppliers will be willing to sell; and producers of *A* will be able to operate their higher-cost plants at a profit, run their factories harder, and pay overtime wages and higher prices for necessary materials. More generally, as production increases, marginal costs rise; i.e., the cost of producing additional units increases. As a consequence, to produce at higher levels, producers must be paid a higher price for their product. In sum, in a typical situation, *the higher the price offered, the more will be supplied*. The supply curve reflects this condition. As the price rises, more is supplied, as indicated by the supply curve sloping upward to the right.

[7]Readers who have studied price theory may wish to skip this section. See the books in this Series by R. Dorfman, *Prices and Markets* and *The Price System*, for full discussions of these topics.

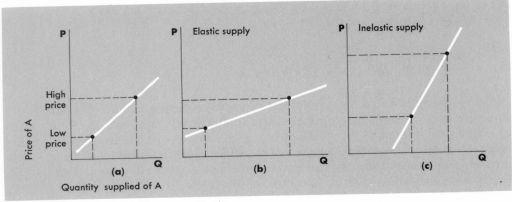

FIG. 1–4  Supply curves

For some commodities, a small increase in price will result in a large increase in the amount suppliers are willing to sell (Fig. 1–4b). We refer to this as a case of elastic supply. In other cases, even a considerable increase in price will produce only a small additional supply (Fig. 1–4c). This is an example of inelastic supply. Whether the supply for a particular commodity is elastic or inelastic depends upon production costs, the size of stocks in the hands of suppliers, the expectations of future price trends, and a wide variety of other factors. In general, the elasticity of supply becomes greater the longer the period allowed for adjustment: if the price of $A$ rises today, some additional supply will be coaxed out of potential suppliers' present holdings, but production cannot respond overnight; if the price increase persists, production will be increased as firms find it profitable to bring higher-cost standby capacity into use and to pay overtime.

Among the potential buyers, a higher price will also lead to a response different from that generated by a low price. The cheaper a commodity, the more of it will be bought. More buyers will be willing to spend their money on this commodity rather than on another. And each buyer may wish to purchase a larger quantity if the price is low.

Figure 1–5a shows a typical demand curve. The lower the price of a commodity, the more of it is demanded. The elastic demand curve of Fig. 1–5b corresponds to a commodity where demand is highly sensitive to price, such as the case of a material for which there are close substitutes. The inelastic demand curve (Fig. 1–5c) might be for a commodity such as salt, for which there are no substitutes.

Given the supply and demand curves, it is possible to determine the equilibrium price for commodity $A$. Figure 1–6 shows the two curves on one diagram. At the point $E$, where price is equal to $P_1$, the potential buyers demand $b$ units. At that same price, the potential sellers are willing to supply $b$ units. Thus, at

20

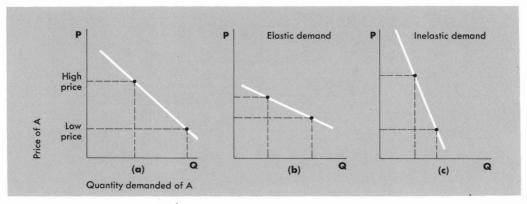

FIG. 1–5   Demand curves ⟩ ✳

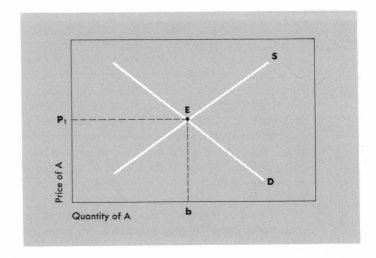

FIG. 1–6   Supply, demand, and
equilibrium price

that price the number of units that people wish to sell equals the number of units that others wish to buy: $P_1$ is the price that precisely clears the market. It is the *equilibrium price*.

Suppose the price is lower, say $P_0$ in Fig. 1–7. Then the potential buyers will demand $c$ units, but the sellers will be willing to sell only $d$ units, thus creating an excess demand of $dc$. This excess demand will exert upward pressure on the price. The sellers will see that buyers are attempting to buy more units than they are putting on the market, and they will respond by raising the price.

Suppose the price is at $P_2$, above the equilibrium price. Then the sellers

21

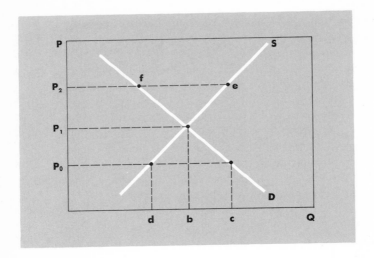

FIG. 1–7 Excess demand and excess supply

will be attempting to sell *e* units, while the buyers will be willing to purchase only *f* units. This makes for an excess supply of *fe*, which will exert downward pressure on the price. The sellers will be left with unwanted inventories. They will realize that they can move these inventories only if they lower the price. After some period of adjustment, the price will tend to settle at the equilibrium price $P_1$.

The supply and demand curves do not remain static. Costs of production may change; consumer tastes may change. And consumer incomes will gradually rise over time, enabling people to buy more of most commodities at any given price. Such changes will be reflected by shifts of the demand and supply curves. For example, the invention of a cost-cutting production technique may shift the entire supply curve to the right. Higher incomes may shift demand curves to the right.

In the real world, both the demand and supply curves shift constantly. It may well be that the precise equilibrium price is never reached because the price adjustments never quite catch up to the newly emerging excess demands or excess supplies. But even if never reached, the equilibrium price plays a strategic role in economic analysis. It indicates where economic forces are headed at any moment, toward what level the price is moving.

Most of our society's choices about what kinds of goods shall be produced and distributed are made through the operations of demand and supply in the market. Earlier, you will recall, we pointed out that rational choice involves a comparison between the values that society places on different goods and the marginal opportunity costs of producing those goods. The forces of demand and supply are the means by which information about values and costs are transmitted and acted upon. Demand curves reflect information about values. Supply curves reflect information about marginal costs. From the point of view of society, production of a particular good in its equilibrium quantity at least roughly represents a rational choice based upon comparison of values and marginal costs. Precisely how demand and supply curves relate to social values and marginal costs, and how the concepts of equilibrium and rational choice are related to each other, form one of the major aspects of micro-economics. Not all markets are perfect, of course. The demand curves for a particular good may reflect consumer misinformation and the supply curve may be distorted by monopoly elements. Part of micro-economics, therefore, deals with imperfect markets and what can be done to make them more perfect.

As we shall see in the succeeding chapters, these ideas of the demand, supply, and equilibrium are also useful in analyzing the economy as a whole. In particular, the relation between the economy's aggregate supply of goods and services and its aggregate demand for them is crucial in determining the extent of unemployment or of inflation that the nation experiences.

## WHY ECONOMISTS OFTEN DISAGREE

A common complaint about economics that is voiced by many people —not excluding students in the Principles of Economics course—might be expressed as follows: "You economists purport to be a professional group. You use complicated terminology, mathematics, statistics, and the whole paraphernalia of scientific inquiry. Yet, when it comes to a specific issue of national economic policy, you can seldom agree among yourselves. And even when you do, you often can't seem to convince enough of your fellow citizens to follow your advice —which, anyway, sometimes appears to fly in the face of common sense."

Most of the subjects with which economics deals have important implications for national policy. What is the role of competition in achieving our high living standards? To what extent does the existence of a few giant firms in an industry—the big three in autos, for example—violate the competitive ideal, and how is this situation affected by the antitrust laws? What would be the effect of a reduction in taxes paid by upper-income groups on the level of output, on the growth of output, or on income distribution? How does a farm subsidy affect farm income, consumer prices, and national income? Is a federal budget deficit always an undesirable state of affairs, always a desirable state of affairs, or sometimes one and sometimes the other? About these, and almost all the policy questions with which economics deals, you can find eminent public officials, and in many cases eminent economists, taking opposing positions.

Does economics, then, have a claim to being anything more than an organized way of presenting firmly held prejudices? Are there, in other words, such things as "principles" of economics that are generally accepted and are in some sense neutral with respect to partisan politics? If such principles do exist, why then do we so often find economists unable to agree unanimously on many policy

23

questions, as we might expect a group of physicists to agree on a body of specific principles relating, say, to the forces of gravitation and inertia acting on an orbiting satellite?

A full treatment of these problems would require a volume in itself. And, in any event, the best way to gain an appreciation of the scope and limits of economics as a discipline is to study its specific content. But there are a few basic points to make at the very beginning.

### Differences in Social Values

As we said before, a large part of economics consists of the study of *choice*. The allocation of scarce resources among competing uses, for example, forces us, as a society, to make choices. Economics cannot tell us that Shakespeare is a better source of reading material than comic books, or that we ought to devote more of our national resources to upgrading the quality of education and less to the production of cosmetics and tobacco. Rather, economics takes our tastes and preferences as given and attempts, first, to explain how the economic system turns out goods and services in response to our preferences; and second, what improvements in the price system or in our governmental expenditure policy might make the system respond more efficiently. Hence, when one economist testifies before a congressional committee that government spending on education ought to be increased, and the next witness, also an economist, says that government spending is already too high and private spending too low, there is no necessary disagreement on economic principles involved. Rather, the two economists disagree on the values which, as individual citizens, they assign to the worth of additional spending on education.

Take, as another example, a proposal to reduce the progressiveness of the tax system—say, to lower the tax rates on upper incomes and to raise the level of sales taxes that fall most heavily on lower-income groups. Two economists might well agree on an analysis of the economic effects—on total income and output, on economic growth, and on income distribution. Yet one might well oppose the reduction because as an individual he felt that the distribution of income was already too heavily loaded in favor of wealthy taxpayers, whereas the other might endorse the reduction because he felt that equalization of income had already been carried too far.

In other words, much of the disagreement among economists on particular policy measures exists not so much because they can't agree on economic principles but because, as individual citizens, they put different values on social objectives. Their disagreements are not so much economic as they are social or political.

### Economics and the Physical Sciences

In many cases economists can agree on the *general* effects of a given policy, but not on the *specific* magnitude or timing of those effects. Most economists would agree, for example, that a reduction in corporate income taxes would stimulate business investment in new plant and equipment, and in turn raise the rate of growth in national output and productivity. But by how much? Many would argue that the stimulus to investment per one billion dollars of tax cut would be quite small and the impact on growth would be minimal. They would feel that the reduction in tax revenues and the necessity, under conditions of full employment, to compensate by raising other taxes or reducing government expenditures would be too great a price to pay for a very small increase in the rate of growth. On the other hand, an economist who felt that a moderate cut in corporate taxes would furnish a sharp stimulus to investment and growth might espouse such a tax cut. In these kinds of situations the differences among economists stem not from differences in social values or in fundamental economic principles, but from inability to agree on an estimate of the quantitative effect of the measure, in this case the amount of investment per dollar of tax reduction.

But why should it be so difficult to agree on measuring the impact of economic policies? After all, taxes, income, output, employment, and the like, are all measurable quantities. The difficulty stems from a number of factors.

*First*: Unlike physicists, economists cannot conduct controlled experiments. If a physicist wishes to test the electrical conductivity of different sizes of copper wire, he can control the specific size and quality of the wire, the temperature of the laboratory, and the current passing through the wire. He can, in other words, keep constant everything but the factor he is observing—the different sizes of wire—and observe what happens when he changes this one factor. But an economist cannot do this. We do not—and no one suggests that we should—change economic policy simply to observe the effects of change. Even if we did, we couldn't keep other things constant. In 1964, for example, taxes were lowered and the economy entered on a strong period of expansion. But we can't simply observe what happened to the economy in the next two years and say that all changes were due to the tax cut. Many other things were changing also. In general, we have to take the economy as the complicated, interacting, continuously changing phenomenon that it is and attempt to derive our measurements under those conditions. The gradual development of advanced statistical techniques and the more recent revolution in data handling through high-speed computers have enabled economists to make broad strides to obtain reliable measurements of some important economic relationships. But we will never attain the precision of the natural sciences.

*Second*: Electrons, at least in large numbers, behave according to regular predictable patterns. Human beings, considered in large numbers, also follow certain behavior patterns. But the patterns are more complicated and much less predictable than those exhibited by physical phenomena; moreover, they change gradually and—occasionally quite swiftly—over time. As a consequence, the response of groups and individuals to economic events is not constant over the years.

In summary, economics *is* less precise in its findings than the natural sciences; it deals with human society, which has always been, and hopefully always will be, more diverse, full of more surprises, and less predictable than natural phenomena. We do not have nice neat equations that will yield answers for all situations. Nevertheless, there *are* objective principles of economics that can be applied. More important, the study of economics can furnish us with an objective method of analysis, so that in dealing with questions of economic growth and stability we need not remain mere slaves to hoary slogans or prejudices.

## SUMMARY

Economics deals with the ways a society utilizes its scarce resources of manpower, raw materials, and capital to satisfy the material wants of its members. This classical definition is incomplete, however. It does not fully reflect two of the major concerns of modern economics: growth and instability.

Over the past several centuries *economic growth* has been a central characteristic of Western economies. The output of goods and services, in terms of both quantity and quality, has increased much more rapidly than population, leading to a manifold rise in living standards. As a general rule—and particularly in the last half-century—this increase in living standards has been widely shared among the population.

Sustained economic growth requires continual change in the techniques and organization of production. Old methods give way to new and yesterday's goods are displaced by today's. As a consequence, the process of growth requires adaptation, and adaptation is painful. As old industries die, to be replaced by new, some people and occasionally whole areas suffer from unemployment and economic blight. Measures that assist people and communities to adapt to change can also promote economic growth. Attempts to eliminate economic insecurity by placing roadblocks in the way of technological change slow down economic growth and in the long run are a poor solution to the problem.

In addition to the specific pockets of unemployment left in the wake of economic progress, Western economies have been subject to the periodic occurrence of *mass unemployment*. Mass unemployment and depression stem not from the economy's inability to produce but from an inability to sell what can be produced by a fully employed labor force. In analyzing the problem of economic instability, therefore, we must distinguish between actual production and potential production. When market demand falls short of potential production, unemployment occurs. When, on the other hand, market demand runs ahead of the economy's productive potential, inflation results. Economic growth is an expansion of potential output; economic instability is the fluctuation of actual output relative to potential.

In the modern interdependent economy, economic activity resembles a circular flow. Business firms hire workers; they buy raw materials, plant, and equipment; they produce goods. The costs the firms incur in producing the goods take the form of incomes to workers and investors. These incomes in turn buy the goods that business firms produce. Production generates income; incomes are spent to purchase production.

When an economy is producing at capacity, it generates sufficient income to purchase all the goods produced. If all income received by workers and investors is spent directly or indirectly to purchase goods, then a market will exist for total output. But if spending falls short of potential output, firms will not continue to produce at the same level. Output will fall, unemployment will appear, and plants will not operate at full capacity. The forces that produce fluctuations in output and lead to alternating periods of prosperity and depression are thus to be found in the relation between production, income, and spending.

## A PREVIEW

If we wish to study the growth and stability of national output and income, we must first understand the meaning of output and income and how they are measured. In Chapter 2, therefore, we examine the definition and measurement of national output and income and their various components. The next three chapters deal with the problem of economic instability. In Chapters 3 and 4 we analyze the factors that determine the actual level of national output. Under what conditions will actual output be less than potential output? What are some of the important measures that can be used to prevent major declines in economic activity or to reverse them once they have occurred? Whereas Chapters 3 and 4 concentrate on one aspect of economic instability—depression and unemployment—Chapter 5 is devoted to examining the opposite aspect of economic instability—namely, inflation. Finally, in Chapter 6, we return to the question of economic growth and attempt to discover the important forces that cause a nation's economic potential to expand. With the material in Chapters 2 through 5 behind us, we shall be able to see that the problems of economic growth and economic stability are interrelated. Some of the very features of our economy that lead to growth may also make it susceptible to economic instability. Conversely, failure to hold economic fluctuations within reasonable limits may slow down, or even halt, economic growth.

# National Output

# and Income

## CHAPTER TWO

The end result of economic activity is the production of goods and services and the distribution of those goods and services to the members of society. All the branches of economics are concerned in one way or another with output and income. In order to evaluate the performance of our economic system—in terms of how rapidly it is growing, how stable it is, or how it allocates its productive resources to different end products—we need some measure of output and income. Strangely enough, however, it was not until the 1930s that reliable over-all figures on national output and income were first produced. In part this was because comprehensive data were hard to come by. A more important reason, however, was that up until the 1930s most economists concerned themselves not so much with the over-all performance of the economy (i.e., macro-economics) but with the price system and the allocation of resources (i.e., micro-economics). The coming of the Great Depression of the 1930s forced economists to devote attention to the over-all level of economic activity. The economic problem of the time was the depressed level of production and employment. In order to pursue analysis in this direction, to measure the depth of the depression and the extent of recovery, it was necessary to construct data on national output and income.[1]

[1]The most important pioneer in providing national income data was Professor Simon Kuznets, for the National Bureau of Economic Research, a private research organization. In the late 1930s and during World War II, the official national income estimates of the U.S. government were developed in the Department of Commerce, which has continued to provide annual and quarterly estimates since then. In the postwar period the development of systems of national income data has spread from the industrial countries throughout the world. One

The data on national output and income, and their components, are published by the U.S. Department of Commerce in the form of a set of *national income accounts.* These accounts supply the most valuable data we have about our economy. Are we interested in forecasting the level of economic activity next year? The national income accounts provide a quantified framework of output, spending, and income on which to base our forecast. Do we wish to study long-term economic growth? The historical data in the national income accounts show how rapidly output has grown in the past, how its growth compared with population or labor force growth, and what proportion of output has been devoted to growth-stimulating investment. Are we concerned about the distribution of income between wages and profits? The data to make such comparisons are found in that part of the accounts dealing with the components of income.

## GROSS NATIONAL PRODUCT
## AND GROSS NATIONAL INCOME

The most comprehensive measure of national output is the *gross national product,* usually abbreviated GNP.

*The GNP is the value of all goods and services produced annually in the nation.*

In terms of Fig. 1–1, p. 9, GNP is the flow of total production in the upper half of the loop. Notice that GNP is a *flow*; it is an amount of production per unit of time. By convention, we measure GNP in terms of annual flows. This is similar to our convention of measuring the speed of an automobile in miles per hour.

The circular flow diagram brings out another important fact about GNP. Production flows generate income flows; the flow of gross national product is matched by a flow of *gross national income (GNI),* the lower half of the loop.

*GNI, therefore, is the sum of all of the incomes* (wages, profits, rent, interest, etc.) *earned in the production of GNP. GNI is always equal to GNP.*

As a consequence, there are at least two ways of measuring GNP: first, we can sum up the value of goods and services produced; second, we can estimate GNI by summing up the value of incomes created in the process of producing those goods and services. Since GNI = GNP, conceptually, both techniques yield

---

of the first tasks in stimulating economic growth among the less-developed nations has been the building of national income accounting structures, within the framework of which an economy's resources and capabilities can be evaluated. The United Nations has formulated a standard system of national income accounting around which many nations develop their own national income data.

the same answer. Both sets of data are provided by the U.S. Department of Commerce in its national income accounts. As estimated, they do sometimes show small differences because of incomplete measurement. Table 2–1 shows the major components of GNP and GNI for 1969.

Table 2–1  TWO MEASURES OF GNP IN 1969

(Billions of Current Dollars)

| Final Output (GNP) | | Incomes Generated (GNI) | |
|---|---|---|---|
| Consumption | $576 | Compensation of Employees | $564 |
| Investment | 139 | Interest | 31 |
| Government purchases | 215 | Rent | 22 |
| Net exports | 2 | Corporate profits | 88 |
| | | Unincorporated business income | 66 |
| | | Depreciation | 78 |
| | | Other incomes | 83 |
| | | (mostly property and sales taxes received by government) | |
| Total GNP | $932 | Total GNI | $932 |

## THE VALUATION OF OUTPUT

We have defined GNP as the total value of goods and services produced annually in the nation. But literally hundreds of thousands of different kinds of goods and services make up the GNP. How can we add automobiles to symphony concerts, frozen food to doctors' services, pencil sharpeners to vacation trips? The answer is given by the term value. To each good or service we assign a relative importance or value, given by its price. An automobile sold for $3,000 is counted in the GNP as $3,000; a seat in the bleachers for a baseball game, priced at $2, is counted in GNP as $2. In other words, each good or service is multiplied by its price, and the resultant dollar values total GNP.

Notice the implications of this procedure. It assumes that the relative importance of a particular good is given by its relative price. Automobiles are ascribed an importance 1,500 times that of bleacher seats at a ball game; a suit of clothes at $60 is weighted 40 times greater than a six-pack of beer at $1.50. Insofar as the prices that consumers are willing to pay for different goods reflect the amount of satisfaction they get from additional units of output of those goods, then GNP, in some rough sense, corresponds to a measurement of the economic worth of production to society. Individual choices, made by millions of consumers and businessmen, give us the relative measure of value. But what about those societies —for example, the Soviet Union—in which prices are set by the government to carry out its objectives? This difference in pricing systems makes a meaningful comparison of over-all Russian GNP figures with ours difficult. Even in our own

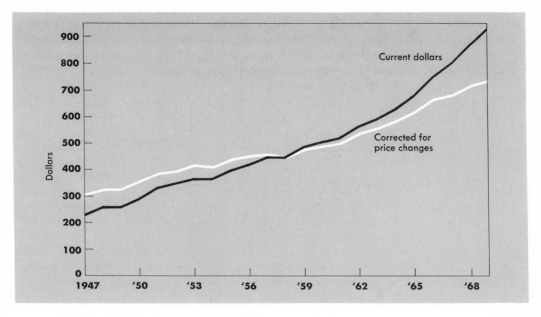

FIG. 2–1  GNP in current and constant (1958) dollars, 1947–1969

country relative prices are not always an accurate reflection of the value of different goods to consumers. Most government services, such as the defense contribution of our armed forces, are not sold at a price. In this case we have to be satisfied with a cruder method of valuation—the cost of inputs needed to produce such services.

### Adjusting for Changes in the Price Level

When prices change, the values (or "weights") assigned to the various goods and services in GNP also change. Thus, in an inflation the prices of most goods are rising, and the value of GNP increases simply because of the price rise. To determine how much *real* output has changed, we must first adjust for the effect of changes in prices, so that any increase in GNP reflects a rise in output, not the rise in prices. The way in which economists adjust for changes in prices is conceptually very simple (but in practice quite difficult). Each year the value of each kind of output is expressed in terms of the prices prevailing in some single base year. The result is a series of GNP values in *constant dollars*. Constant dollar GNP (often called "deflated GNP") measures changes in real output, since each component of GNP, in each year, is valued at the unchanged prices of the base year. The difference between current dollar and deflated GNP is quite considerable (see Fig. 2–1). The annual rate of increase of current dollar GNP

31

averaged 6.5 per cent from 1947 to 1969. Corrected for price increases, the deflated GNP rose by only 3.9 per cent a year. During some depressions since World War II, current dollar GNP has risen while real GNP fell. Between 1957 and 1958, for example, real GNP fell by about 1 per cent. But prices rose 2.5 per cent. Current dollar GNP, therefore, rose by 1.5 per cent.

### Avoiding Double-Counting

The task of estimating the GNP would seem to consist merely of adding up the value of all output, the value of any particular output being equal to the quantity produced (e.g., 9 million automobiles) times the average price per unit (e.g., $3,000). Things are not quite this simple, however. Take a loaf of bread priced at 20 cents, for example (see Fig. 2–2). To produce the loaf of bread, the baker purchased 11 cents worth of flour, baked it into bread, and sold the bread for 20 cents. The flour miller in turn purchased wheat for 6 cents and milled it into flour, selling the flour for 11 cents. The farmer supplied the 6 cents worth of wheat to the miller, and himself purchased fertilizer and seed from other industries. Query: In estimating GNP, do we add up value of bread, flour, wheat, and fertilizer to a total of 38 cents? Clearly not. *We would be double-counting, since the value of the flour is already included in the 20-cent price for bread, as is the value of the wheat, the fertilizer, and the seed. In order to avoid this double-counting, we add only the value of final output—i.e., the goods and services sold to final users during the period.* In Fig. 2–2, for example, it is the 20-cent value of the bread that enters the GNP. We are not excluding the output of flour and wheat from our GNP total. Since their value is incorporated in the price of the bread, our rule about counting only the final products still embraces the entire value of the output.

Figure 2–2 also shows the two approaches to measuring GNP. On the one hand, the value of final output (20 cents) can be measured; on the other, the income generated in each industry can be added up. Either approach avoids double-counting and yields a reliable estimate of GNP (= GNI).

The two approaches must supply the same answer: For example, the sum of all incomes generated in producing the bread will exactly equal the value of the bread. Even if the wages and other costs paid out in producing the bread were greater than its price, total income would still equal the value of output! Why? Because *profits* are the balancing item. If, for example, the sum of what the baker paid out for flour, wages, and other costs were greater than 20 cents, his profits would be *negative* by an amount exactly equal to the difference. Consequently, when we add all the incomes, including profits, the total would still be exactly 20 cents.[2]

[2]There is a third method of calculating national output. We can total the *value added* to final output by each industry. Value added is simply the difference between the sales of a firm and its purchases from other firms. In Fig. 2–2, the value added in the baking industry is 9 cents (20 cents worth of sales minus an 11-cent purchase of flour). The sum of value added by all industries equals the value

| Product | Sales | Value added by each industry | Income generated (wages, profits, etc.) |
|---|---|---|---|
| Bread | 20¢ (value of output) ↦ Baking industry . . . . . | 9¢ | 9¢ |
| Flour | 11¢ ↦ Milling industry . . . . . | 5¢ | 5¢ |
| Wheat | 6¢ ↦ Agriculture . . . . . . | 5¢ | 5¢ |
| Fertilizer, seed, etc. | 1¢ ↦ Chemical industry, etc. . . | 1¢ | 1¢ |
| Totals | 38¢ | 20¢ | 20¢ |

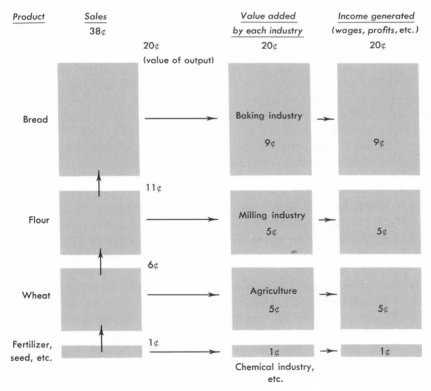

**FIG. 2–2** The value of output equals the value of income

of final output, and hence equals GNP. Moreover, in each industry, value added (sales minus purchases) also equals the value of income created (GNI). In a complex industrial society there are very few final outputs produced solely by one industry. The final value of any product is created by a large number of different industries; each firm buys materials or supplies from other firms, processes or transports them, and thus adds to their value.

When we say that GNP is equal to the total value of goods and services produced in the nation, precisely what do we mean? Granted that we include only final goods and services—to avoid double-counting—are there any other limitations on what is to be encompassed in our summation? Clearly, yes. The GNP, after all, is meant to be a measure of the output of our *economic system*. We undertake many activities that result in "output" of some kind or another, but that are not economic in nature. When I go home from work, I may spend my leisure time gardening or making furniture. Are the vegetables or shelves I produce to be included in GNP, like commercial products? No, because these are not economically oriented activities. They are the product of leisure time, pursued for their own sake and not, generally, for their economic value.

In a modern economic society the major way to distinguish what is economic production from what is essentially a hobby, or a part of the ordinary routine of running a home, is to ask, "Does it go through the market place—is it sold?" This is generally the criterion used in deciding whether a particular kind of activity is *economic* output and therefore to be included in GNP. Even though the criterion of the market place is sensible, it sometimes leads to apparently strange results. For example, if I spend my evenings for a year building a new room for my house, the value of my labor is *not* included in the GNP, but the value of the lumber, nails, and paint purchased from the local hardware dealer is counted. Those of us who are likely to hammer more thumbs than nails would have to have the whole job contracted if we wanted (and could afford!) a new room; in this case the entire cost of the room, including the wages and profit of the builder, would be included in GNP, because the entire transaction was economic in nature. Similarly, the wages of domestic servants represent "services" produced and as such add to the GNP. But the same services performed "non-economically" by the housewife are not part of GNP. This anomaly led one eminent English economist to remark that the man who married his housekeeper would reduce the national income.

Despite these borderline cases, the application of the market criterion generally does what was intended—it restricts GNP to a measure of economic output. There are a few cases, however, in which the blind application of this rule would lead to absurd results. So the rule is occasionally relaxed. The farmer's consumption of food grown on his own farm is one example. The most important exception, however, relates to the owner-occupied home. The rental value of housing forms part of the GNP. Rent represents the value of "shelter" produced; it is produced by scarce resources (the materials, labor, and capital embodied in the house) and as such is a part of the national output. But in the United States today only about 40 per cent of all dwelling units are rented from landlords; the other 60 per cent are owned by the occupants. It would indeed be peculiar to count the rent paid to the landlord as part of the GNP and ignore the rental value provided by owner-occupied housing. Owning a home is an economic matter. It is a businesslike investment, even if there is no payment of rent to a landlord. Consequently, the national income statistics include an estimate of the rental value of owner-occupied housing. In effect, the homeowner is treated as a landlord renting to himself.

*exception to rules*

## THE MAJOR USES OF GNP

There are four major components of final output in the GNP, classified by the type of use to which output is put: *consumption, investment, government purchases,* and *net exports*. All output flows to one of these four uses. Their sum is therefore equal to GNP and encompasses all output produced in the nation.

*components of GNP*

| Consumption |

Consumer expenditures currently absorb about 62 per cent of final output. In the 1920s they represented some 75 per cent; the growth of defense expenditures (from about 1 per cent of GNP in 1929 to 8 per cent in 1969) and of other public expenditures has been mainly at the expense of consumption.

The three kinds of consumer expenditures and their growth since 1929 are shown in Table 2–2. Notice how very differently each of the three major categories of consumer expenditures reacted to the Great Depression of the 1930s. By 1932, the low point of the depression, total consumer expenditures had fallen 17 per cent from their 1929 level. But durables declined 48 per cent, whereas purchases of services and nondurable goods fell only 13 and 15 per cent, respectively. Durable-goods purchases generally can be postponed when income declines and unemployment threatens; the old car can last another year, appliance and furniture purchases can be delayed. But outlays for food, rent, and doctors'

*Durable goods
non durable goods
services*

Table 2–2  THE GROWTH OF CONSUMER EXPENDITURES

(Billions of Constant, 1958 Dollars)

| Category | 1929 | 1932 | 1969 | Percentage Change 1929 to 1932 | Percentage Change 1929 to 1969 |
|---|---|---|---|---|---|
| Consumption | $140 | $115 | $466 | −18% | +233% |
| Durable goods | 16 | 8 | 85 | −48 | +431 |
| Nondurable goods | 69 | 60 | 199 | −13 | +188 |
| Services | 54 | 46 | 182 | −15 | +237 |

Notice that this is a table in constant 1958 dollars; consumption goods in each year are valued at 1958 prices. That is why the $466 billion shown for total consumption in 1969 is less than the $576 billion shown in Table 2–1, where goods are valued in terms of the higher prices of 1969.

bills have to be continued, even if this means dipping into past savings or borrowing. Over the entire period from 1929 to 1969 consumer purchases of durable goods rose much more rapidly than other purchases, followed by services, and nondurable goods lost their traditional share of the consumer's dollar.

/ Investment /

Part of the nation's output is devoted not to meeting consumer wants, but to building the economy's plants and equipment. Just as an individual family may choose to forego current consumption and use the resultant saving to earn future income, so a nation can expand its productive potential by using part of its resources to produce plant, equipment, housing, and other productive assets. It thus provides the capital goods that, together with a skilled labor force and technological progress, make possible abundant production and rising living standards.

The term "investment" as used in the national income accounts has a precise meaning that is not always the same as its everyday use. For example, I may consider my purchase of a share of stock in General Motors as an investment. However, this transaction in itself does *not* represent investment from the nation's point of view. My purchase of a security does not add any machinery or plant to the nation's wealth. Rather, it is merely a transfer of a stock certificate from one owner to another. Similarly, if I purchase an already existing home, this indeed is an investment from my point of view, but only a change in the ownership of an existing asset from a national point of view: my "investment" in the house is matched by the former owner's "disinvestment." *Investment, as a category of GNP, is that part of current output which takes the form of additions to or replacements of real productive assets.*

Total gross investment fulfills two purposes. Each year part of the value of the total capital in use is lost. Machines and factories gradually wear out and newer methods of production make existing equipment obsolete. Consequently, each year new machinery and plants must be produced and installed, merely to maintain the existing stock of capital—to offset the depreciation of capital. The remainder of investment represents net additions to the stock of productive capital. *Net investment, therefore, is equal to gross investment less depreciation.*

*1969 Investment, Gross and Net*

| Gross Investment | $131 billion |
|---|---|
| Less: Depreciation | 79 billion |
| Net Investment | 52 billion |

It is important not to confuse the various terms used in connection with investment. *Capital* represents the *total stock* of productive assets in existence at any point in time: plant, equipment, housing, trucks, ships, etc. *Gross investment* is the amount of those assets produced each year and used either (1) to replace

36

that part of the stock of capital that has worn out and deteriorated over the year, or (2) to increase the stock of capital. This latter amount is called *net investment*. The increase in the stock of capital in any one year is, therefore, precisely equal to the net investment of that year.

A nation whose annual gross investment is equal only to depreciation is not adding to its productive capacity. Indeed, unless gross investment at least equals depreciation, net investment will be negative, and the nation's capital stock will decrease. Only as net investment is positive will the stock of productive assets grow.

There are three major categories of investment in the GNP accounts:

1. *Business fixed investment* consists of both single-family dwellings and tal assets, such as machinery, factory buildings, offices, and stores.

2. *Residential construction* consists of both single-family dwellings and apartments and may be for rental or for occupancy by homeowners. (The purchase of a new home by an individual family is classified in the national income accounts as an investment rather than a consumption purchase because it represents the purchase of a major productive asset, and the mere fact that the purchase is made by an individual rather than a business firm does not make it any less an investment.)

3. *Change in business inventories* (or "inventory investment") is the part of output that is absorbed by business firms as an increase in their stocks of finished goods, goods-in-process, and raw materials. The total output of any year is either sold to final users (consumers, investors, government, exporters) or used to build up inventories, and we must be sure to count both uses of output in GNP. *Final output includes both sales to final users and the change in business inventories.*

Inventory change can be positive or negative. If inventories are decreasing, as in Case I of Table 2–3, sales to final users are greater than output. Some part

**Table 2–3   INVENTORIES, SALES, AND OUTPUT: AN EXAMPLE**

(Billions of Dollars)

| | | |
|---|---|---|
| **Case I.** Decrease in inventories: Sales exceed output | | |
| 1. Sales to final users | | $560 |
| Inventories at beginning of period | 90 | |
| Inventories at end of period | 85 | |
| 2. Change in inventories | | −5 |
| 3. Total Output = GNP = | | $555 |
| **Case II.** Increase in inventories: Output exceeds sales | | |
| 1. Sales to final users | | $560 |
| Inventories at beginning of period | 85 | |
| Inventories at end of period | 90 | |
| 2. Change in inventories | | +5 |
| 3. Total Output = GNP = | | $565 |

37

of sales is not coming from current production but out of existing inventories of goods on hand. Therefore, in order to calculate output (GNP), we must subtract from the total of final sales the decrease in inventories. If, on the other hand, inventories are increasing, as in Case II, some part of output is not flowing to final users. In this case, to measure output we must add to final sales the value of output being added to inventories. Of course, it is the *change* in inventories that is relevant to the calculation of GNP, not the level of inventories. No matter how high the level of inventories is, as long as it remains constant it has no effect on GNP. Current output is absorbed by building the stock of inventories, just as it is absorbed by adding to the stock of other kinds of capital like machinery or buildings.

### The Volatility of Investment Expenditures

Table 2–4 summarizes the changes in the major categories of investment since 1929. Notice the dramatic decline in investment during the depression years. While consumer expenditure fell 18 per cent between 1929 and 1932, investment fell 89 per cent! All categories of investment declined, and inventory investment became negative—i.e., business firms were depleting their inventories. Since the capital stock continued to depreciate during the period, the extremely low level of gross investment implied that net investment was negative. In other words, purchases of plant, equipment, and housing were not sufficient to make good the annual wear and tear and the obsolescence that was occurring; hence the nation's capital stock declined significantly during these years.

The volatility of investment expenditures plays the principal role in economic fluctuations. The 1929–1932 experience is an extreme example, to be sure. Nevertheless, investment outlays almost always fluctuate proportionately more than other components of GNP (aside from defense expenditures in wartime). Chapters 3 and 4 will show how fluctuations in investment spending lead to substantial swings in total output and employment and will explain why investment spending has been so volatile.

### Table 2–4  INVESTMENT EXPENDITURES, SELECTED YEARS
(Billions of Constant, 1958 Dollars)

| | | | | Percentage Change | |
| | | | | 1929 to 1932 | 1929 to 1969 |
| Category | 1929 | 1932 | 1969 | | |
| --- | --- | --- | --- | --- | --- |
| Total gross investment | $40.4 | $4.6 | $111 | −89% | +175% |
| Business fixed investment | 26.5 | 8.1 | 81 | −69 | +206 |
| Producers' durable equipment | 12.6 | 3.8 | 57 | −70 | +352 |
| Nonresidential construction | 13.9 | 4.3 | 24 | −69 | + 73 |
| Residential construction | 10.4 | 2.7 | 23 | −74 | +121 |
| Change in business inventories | 3.5 | −6.2 | 7 | — | +100 |

**Government**

When the government purchases a missile, pays a private contractor to con-struct a school building, or hires a statistician to measure GNP, it is purchasing an economic good (missiles, buildings) or a service (the work of the statistician). These *government purchases of goods and services* absorb output and are part of GNP.

A significant part of government expenditures does not represent purchases of goods and services; such outlays are *transfer payments*—veterans' pensions, social security benefits, relief payments, and unemployment compensation are a few important examples. These payments are a transfer of income among the members of the society, from the taxpayers to the beneficiaries. They do not represent the purchase of output and are consequently *excluded from the gross national product.*

> transfer payments not part of GNP

Since 1929, government purchases of goods and services have increased more rapidly than any other major component of GNP (see Table 2–5). Of the $67 billion rise in federal purchases of goods and services between 1929 and 1969, about $52 billion was the increase in military purchases. At the state and local levels, the pressure of an expanding population and the postwar movement to the suburbs led to sharp increases in spending on schools, highways, water, and other public services. Part of federal, state, and local government spending represents investment in productive assets that contribute to the capacity and efficiency of the economy. In the United States national income accounts, how-ever, unlike those of most foreign countries, public investment is not included in the investment category of GNP.

**Net Exports**

*Exports* of goods and services are a final use of GNP and must be included in our total. However, some of the purchases of consumers, business, and govern-

**Table 2–5**  GOVERNMENT EXPENDITURES, SELECTED YEARS

(Billions of Constant, 1958 Dollars)

| Category | 1929 | 1947 | 1969 |
|---|---|---|---|
| Government purchases of goods and services | $22 | $40 | $147 |
| Federal | 4 | 19 | 71 |
| State and local | 18 | 21 | 76 |
| Other government expenditures* (primarily transfer payments) | | | |
| Federal | 3 | 23 | 70 |
| State and local | 1 | 2 | 6 |

*Federal and state and local "other" expenditures cannot be added together. Some of the federal expenditures are grants-in-aid to state and local governments, the spending of which is already included in the state and local expenditure totals.

ments are supplied out of *imports* of goods from abroad rather than domestic production. Consequently, our totals of purchases would overstate the value of gross national product produced in the United States. We must therefore subtract purchases of *imported goods and services* from total purchases in order to arrive at a correct total for GNP. In presenting the GNP statistics, this is done by deducting imports from exports, calling the result *net exports*, and showing it as a separate component of GNP. The net export figure is usually a very small proportion of GNP; in 1969 net exports amounted to $2 billion out of a $932-billion GNP total. The $2 billion, however, resulted from a netting of two much larger figures: exports were $55 billion and imports $53 billion.

## GROSS NATIONAL INCOME

Exactly matching the value of goods and services produced, which is GNP, there is a flow of income earned in the production process, which is GNI. A new automobile sold for $3,500 enters the GNP at that value. Correspondingly that $3,500 becomes income to various economic units. Some of it goes to pay the wages and salaries of auto workers and car salesmen. Some of it becomes the profits of auto manufacturers and car dealers. Some of it is used to pay interest on the money borrowed from banks by car manufacturers and dealers. And the federal government, which imposes a manufacturers' excise tax on automobiles, immediately captures some of that $3,500. The value of every good that enters GNP can be broken down into various income components. If we sum all the incomes associated with the production of GNP, we necessarily arrive at a GNI figure that is exactly equal to GNP.[3]

The largest single component of GNI is, as you might expect, *compensation of employees*. In 1969, it accounted for 60 per cent of GNI. Compensation of employees includes wages, salaries, and fringe benefits, such as employer contributions to pension plans. These fringes are part of the cost of production, they are included in the price of commodities and, therefore, in the value of GNP. Consequently, they must also show up in GNI. Compensation of employees is measured before taxes—i.e., not just "take-home" pay is included, but all pay.

The next largest item in GNI is *profits*. Two kinds of profits are included: the profits of corporations and the profits of unincorporated enterprises (including farms). Together, they represented 16 per cent of GNI in 1969. Again these elements of income are measured before taxes. The fact that the government taxes away part of business profits does not make them any less an element of GNI. Profits are the balancing item in GNI. You might wonder, for example,

[3]Although conceptually GNI exactly equals GNP, our statistical estimating techniques are not perfect. Hence, when the national income statisticians actually make independent estimates of the size of GNP and GNI there is always a small difference between the two estimates. This is labeled the *statistical discrepancy*. Statistically, therefore, GNP = GNI + statistical discrepancy.

40

how GNP can always equal GNI since, in some cases, business firms operate at a loss and therefore pay out incomes to workers and others (GNI) that exceed the sales value of the goods produced (GNP). But in such cases, profits are negative by exactly the same amount that incomes paid out exceed the sales value of the goods. An algebraic summation of all incomes, including negative profits, must therefore equal the value of goods sold. GNP will equal GNI.

The next two items of GNI are *interest* and *rent*. Interest is paid on borrowed funds; it is a cost of production and enters into the price of goods sold. The same is true of rent.

*Depreciation* is also a large item in GNI. It represents the deterioration of value in plant and equipment used in the production process. It is an element of cost and is deducted from sales, like other elements of cost, in arriving at a calculation of net profits. Another way to think of this is that a business firm earns a *gross* profit on its sales. Part of this gross profit represents depreciation on its productive assets. The remainder is true net profit.

The final major element of GNI is *indirect business taxes*. Direct taxes are levied on incomes—the individual income tax, the corporate profits tax. But indirect taxes are those that are taken out of the income stream before they enter into incomes. The chief forms of indirect taxes are sales and excise taxes and property taxes. The cost of an automobile to a consumer, for example, includes the excise taxes paid to the federal government and the property taxes paid by car manufacturers and dealers.

## THE FLOW OF GROSS NATIONAL INCOME TO CONSUMERS, BUSINESS, AND GOVERNMENT

Production creates income that leads to spending, which, in turn, calls forth production. It is this circular flow of economic activity that we are seeking to explain. In order to see how the GNP and GNI data fit into the circular flow, however, the income data must be rearranged in a particular way.

Gross national income consists of the sum of earned gross incomes of the individual economic units of the society. But this is not the same as the income available to consumers for spending or saving. First, a part of the total income earned goes to the government as *taxes* of various kinds and is not available for spending by business firms or households. Out of the income I earn as an employee, landlord, or independent businessman, I must pay income taxes—federal, state, and local. Similarly, corporate profits taxes take roughly half of corporate income. Second, corporations retain their depreciation charges and, on the average, about one third of their after-tax profits for reinvestment in the business. This part of gross national income, which we call *gross business saving*, is not available for spending by households. Third, households receive some income

41

that is not generated in the production process and therefore is not included in GNI—namely, *government transfer payments*. The total amount of *disposable personal income* available to consumers is, therefore, equal to gross national income *less* taxes, *less* gross business saving, *plus* transfer payments. We can, in other words, split the total gross national income into three parts, each related to a major spending group in the economy—business, government, and consumers: (1) gross business saving, (2) *net* government taxes (total taxes collected less transfer payments paid out), and (3) disposable personal income (Fig. 2–3).

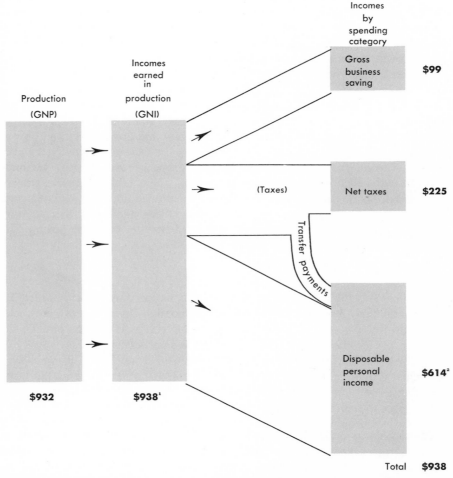

¹ Although GNP and GNI are conceptually equal, there was a $6 billion (0.66 per cent) statistical discrepancy between the two totals when they were estimated independently.

² Excludes "net interest paid by consumers."

**FIG. 2–3** The flow of income to consumer, business, and government

**Gross Business Saving**

*[handwritten margin note: total sales — (costs + interest) = profits + depreciation charges*
*profits — (taxes + dividends) = gross business saving]*

After a corporation pays out its operating costs and the interest on borrowed money, it has left its profits and its depreciation charges. In turn, part of profits are paid to the government in taxes, and another part is paid out as dividends to the stockholders of the corporation. The remainder is "gross business saving," that part of the total flow of income retained by business after payment of taxes and dividends, which it can allocate to various forms of investment.

**Table 2–6  GROSS BUSINESS SAVING**

|  |  | 1969 Values in Billions of Dollars |
|---|---|---|
| Corporate profits | | $88 |
| *Less:* | Corporate profits taxes | 43 |
| | Dividends to stockholders | 24 |
| *Equals:* | Retained profits | 21 |
| *Plus:* | Depreciation | 78 |
| *Equals:* | Gross business saving | 99 |

**Net Taxes**

Government is one of the recipients of gross national income. Almost one third of gross national income goes to federal, state, and local governments in the form of taxes. On the other hand, as we mentioned above, individuals receive transfer payments *from* government, yielding them additional income not included in GNI. Hence the *net* "take" of the government from the income flow is equal to total taxes *less* transfer payments. (see Fig. 2–3).

*[handwritten margin note: net transfer to gov't = total taxes — transfer paym'ts]*

## SPENDING
## AND GROSS NATIONAL INCOME

The income generated in production is eventually divided up into the three major categories—disposable personal income, gross business saving, and net taxes, as shown in Figs. 2–3 and 2–4. In turn, the maintenance of production depends on how the three major spending groups—consumers, investors, and governments—choose to use their income. The juxtaposition of the three GNP categories and the three spending categories in Fig. 2–4, however, does *not* imply that consumption spending equals disposable income, investment equals gross business saving, or government purchases equal net taxes. Normally, for example, consumer expenditures account for only about 90 to 95 per cent of disposable personal income; the other 5 to 10 per cent is saved. Investment, on the other hand, usually *exceeds* gross business saving. Business investment opportunities, in prosperous times, are usually greater than can be financed by retained earnings. Business firms in such situations can tap the savings of individuals by issuing

43

Table 2–7  NET TAXES (FEDERAL, STATE, AND LOCAL)

|  |  | 1969 Values in Billions of Dollars |
|---|---|---|
| Tax Revenues |  | $303 |
| Personal tax payments | $118 |  |
| (income, estate, and gift taxes) |  |  |
| Corporate profits taxes | 43 |  |
| Indirect business taxes | 88 |  |
| (mainly sales and property taxes) |  |  |
| Contributions for social insurance (payroll taxes) | 54 |  |
| *Less:* Transfer payments |  | 78 |
| *Equals:* Net taxes (federal, state, and local) |  | $225 |

securities or by borrowing from financial institutions. And, we well realize, government purchases of goods or services need not be in balance with net tax revenues. When spending exceeds revenue, government finances its deficit by borrowing.

It is precisely to changes in the relationships between spending and income that we must look for the major explanation of depressions and inflation. If spending always represented the same proportion of income in each group, or if

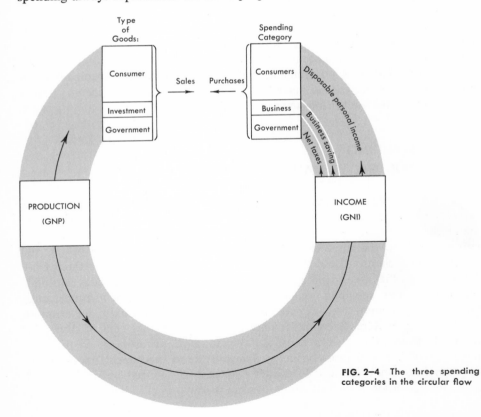

FIG. 2–4  The three spending categories in the circular flow

changes in the spending–income ratio in one group were always exactly offset by opposite changes in the spending patterns of other groups, economic fluctuations would never occur. But spending patterns do change; investment spending tends to fluctuate particularly, leading to instability in production, income, and employment.

## A FAMILY OF INCOME CONCEPTS

Although GNP and GNI, and their divisions into various components, are the key pieces of information for the analysis of circular flow, several other measures of product and income—all subtotals of GNP and GNI—are also useful and applied widely.

_Net national product_ (NNP) is a measure of the net value of total output, corrected for depreciation of the nation's capital stock. After all, part of each year's gross production no more than balances the depreciation of capital. Thus a net measure of all production available for the various end uses, including consumption, government purchases, and additions to the capital stock, is desirable. Net national output is defined as GNP minus depreciation.

_National income_ is equal to net national product _less_ indirect business taxes. That is, in calculating national income we deduct from the total income measure that part of the value of output that represents sales and property taxes. The remainder includes only the incomes of the various factors of production, land, labor, and capital. Hence, national income measures the net value of output in terms of the "factor cost" of producing it.

National income is a particularly good measure of net production because it is not affected by changes in indirect taxes. When sales taxes are increased, both GNP and NNP rise, even though there is no increase in real production. But national income is not affected.[4] National income is the best indicator for making international comparisons of relative income levels.

_Personal income_ is the total income received by households from all sources before taxes. Personal income can be derived from national income by subtracting retained corporate profits, profit taxes, and contributions to social insurance, the three elements of national income that do not reach households. Transfer payments—which are not part of national income because they are not earned

---

[4] National income is the ancestor of all the aggregate income measures. As the total income earned, pioneer statisticians have attempted to measure it at least since 1665, when Sir William Petty computed the national income of England to be 40 million pounds. He estimated that the average person spent about 4½ pence a day for "food housing clothes and other necessaries." That amounts to 6 pounds 13 shillings and 4 pence per year. He estimated the population at 6 million, making for a total outlay of about 40 million pounds. (He assumed that national income equaled annual expense—what we call consumption.)

Today GNP and GNI are the basic measures, because they correspond most closely to the physical volume of production and hence can be estimated more objectively. GNP and GNI do not require precise estimates of depreciation, something that has eluded accountants and economists so far.

by production—have to be added, since they are available to households as a form of income.

*Disposable personal income* is simply personal income after personal taxes. It is the income available to households to spend for consumption or to save. As we have said before, disposable personal income is the flow of GNI that eventually reaches individual households after governments and business firms have taken out taxes and retained profits.

Figure 2–5 is a sophisticated circular flow diagram that relates the several concepts of income and shows how disposable personal income, gross business saving, and net taxes originate in GNP and GNI. If you puzzle through this diagram, you will gain a firm grasp of the structure of the national income accounts.

## POTENTIAL VERSUS ACTUAL GNP

So far in this chapter we have been concerned with the definition and measurement of actual output and income. Equally important, however, is the "potential" or "full employment" level of GNP.

Potential output is that output which *could* be produced if the labor force were fully employed and the industrial capacity fully utilized. "Full employment" does not mean 100 per cent employment. Even in the best of times some workers change jobs and are unemployed while they are looking for new ones. Even in prosperous periods some industries are declining and therefore releasing workers. In general, however, when 96 to 97 per cent of the labor force is employed, and when, on the average, manufacturing plants are operating at 90 to 95 per cent of capacity, we can say that we have full employment and full capacity utilization. These concepts are discussed further in Chapter 6.

Prosperity must be judged by the relations of actual GNP to potential GNP. If the users of final output—consumers, investors, and government, together—do not spend enough to purchase the output that a fully employed economy can produce, then actual output will decline below potential. Workers will be laid off and capacity will be idled. Essentially, then, the central measure of the seriousness of an economic depression is the size of the gap between actual and potential GNP.

## SUMMARY

*Gross national product* is the value of all goods and services produced annually in the nation. For every dollar of GNP produced a dollar of income is created. The sum of all these incomes is the *gross national income*, which is exactly equal to GNP.

Since there are hundreds of thousands of goods and services produced, we must find some common denominator in order to add them together. This com-

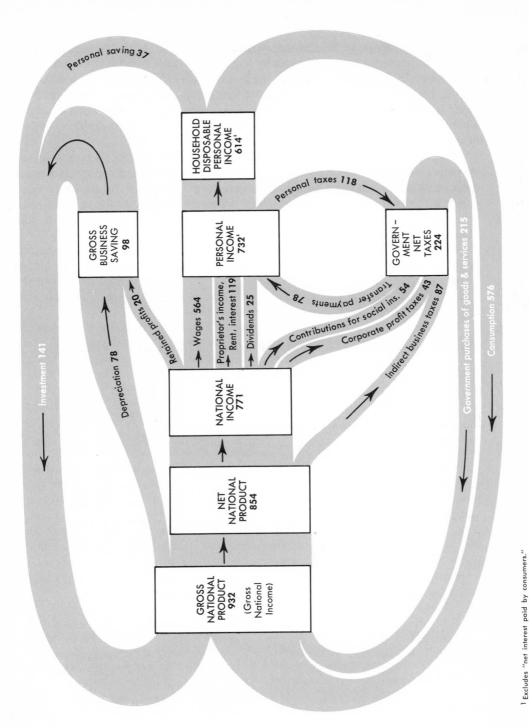

**FIG. 2–5** Income and expenditure flows, 1969 (billions of dollars)

[1] Excludes "net interest paid by consumers."

mon denominator is value. _Each good or service is valued at its market price_. GNP is therefore the sum of the values (price times quantity) of goods and services produced. Prices change, however, and in a period of inflation the value of the GNP would rise simply because prices are rising. To measure changes in _real_ GNP we value each good or service each year in the constant prices of some single base year. The resultant GNP is called _GNP in constant dollars_ (or deflated GNP).

There are two ways of measuring national output. First, we can sum up the value of all _final output_—i.e., goods sold to final users, plus the change in business inventories. We include only final output in order to avoid double-counting. The value of intermediate goods is already included in the value of final output; the value of flour is included in the price of bread, the value of steel in the price of automobiles, and so on.

Second, we can sum up the various incomes earned in the production of final output. This is GNI. Every dollar of final output is matched by a dollar of income generated at some stage or other in the production of that output. GNP equals GNI. Profits are the balancing items in this tabulation since they are the difference between sales receipts and incomes paid out.

There are four major components of GNP, each representing a final use of GNP: consumption, investment, government purchases, and net exports.

Investment in the GNP accounts is that part of final output which takes the form of additions to or replacements of real productive assets. Since part of the nation's stock of productive assets wears out or becomes obsolete each year, part of gross investment must go simply to maintain the stock intact. The remainder, net investment, adds to the stock of productive assets. The investment category of GNP also includes the change in business inventories, which may be positive (output exceeds sales to final users) or negative (output is less than sales to final users). Federal, state, and local government purchases of goods and services are a component of GNP, but governments make other expenditures, transfer payments, which do not represent the purchase of output and are consequently excluded from GNP.

The major components of _gross national income_, as earned, are compensation of employees, profits and depreciation, rent, interest, and indirect business taxes. All the major income items are estimated before taxes. Indirect business taxes are mainly sales, excise, and property taxes, which are not levied on incomes and hence are not included elsewhere in the income components.

The income available to households to spend on consumer goods is not equal to gross national income. Part of this gross national income goes to gross business saving. Another part goes to the government in the form of taxes. On the other hand, households receive income in the form of transfer payments from government which is not a part of GNI. Disposable personal income therefore equals GNI _less_ gross business saving _less_ government taxes _plus_ transfer payments. We can think of the _net_ "take" of the government from the income stream

48

as equal to taxes minus transfer payments. The GNI can then be thought of as flowing into three different income streams—gross business saving, net government taxes, and disposable personal income. Each of these three income streams goes to one of the three main spending groups in the economy: business investors, government, and consumers.

The spending of each of the three major spending groups is not necessarily equal to its income. Indeed, it is precisely in terms of the fluctuation of spending relative to total income generated that we can explain the changes in GNP that lead to recessions and inflations.

Actual GNP is not always equal to potential GNP. Potential GNP is the value of the final output the nation could produce if it operated at reasonably full employment and full utilization of its industrial capacity. When actual GNP is below potential GNP, unemployment and idle plant capacity exist. The size of the gap between actual and potential GNP is a reliable measure of the severity of an economic recession.

# The Determinants
# of Gross National Product

**CHAPTER THREE**

This chapter presents the modern theory of income determination. What factors affect the level of GNP in any given year? What causes GNP to change from year to year? As we have already seen, actual output and income in our economy are not always equal to *potential* output and income. Consequently, we cannot explain the level of GNP merely by referring to the factors that determine how much the economy *can* produce. A theory of income determination must explain how much the economy actually *does* produce—and why actual and potential production often are not the same.

## AGGREGATE DEMAND

Men and factories are involuntarily idle when the goods they are capable of producing cannot be sold. Businessmen will not continue to run their factories at capacity if they cannot sell the output of those factories at a price sufficient to cover their costs (including a reasonable profit). What all business firms taken together can sell depends on the level of *aggregate demand*—i.e., the total volume of purchases that consumers, investors, and government are willing to undertake. If the aggregate demand for goods and services is not sufficient to take off the market the goods that are being produced, business firms will find their inventories mounting rapidly. Faced with the prospect of losses on these excess inventories, firms will reduce output and lay off workers. Total production in the economy, therefore, will tend to adjust to the level of aggregate demand for goods and services. In other words, *subject to the limit set by*

50

*the nation's economic potential, that amount of output will be produced which can profitably be marketed.* If aggregate demand is less than potential GNP, then actual GNP will fall below potential. In the depths of the depression of the 1930s, the nation's productive capacity was little, if any, less than in 1929. The disastrous collapse of production reflected not a reduction in economic potential but a lack of sufficient market demand to make it worthwhile for business firms to use their capacity.

It is easy to understand the failure of a particular firm, or of an industry, to find markets for the output it is capable of producing. Its prices may be too high, the quality of its products may have deteriorated, or consumers may have simply changed their tastes and shifted their allegiance to other products. But why should situations arise in which there is a generalized shortage of spending—a deficiency of aggregate demand—so that the great majority of firms are forced to produce below their capacity and a significant proportion of the labor force cannot find work? After all, we saw in Chapter 2 that the value of gross national product is always exactly matched by the value of gross national income; every dollar of output generates a dollar of income that accrues to some individual or group in the economy. If potential GNP were $950 billion, for example, then the production of that level of GNP would necessarily generate $950 billion of GNI. In turn, if total spending in the economy (aggregate demand) always matched GNI, then there would always be a market for potential GNP—no more, no less. Actual GNP and potential GNP would always be equal. Within the total $950 billion, of course, there might be a number of changes taking place. Some individual firms might be faced with a sales volume far less than their capacity; others might enjoy booming markets that exceeded their capacity. Some firms would be hiring workers and others firing them. But if aggregate demand always equaled GNI, then *total* markets and *total* production would always equal potential GNP.

Therefore, the failure of aggregate demand always to match economic potential and the resulting shortfall in actual production below potential cannot be ascribed to an over-all shortage of income or purchasing power. Production and income are always equal; GNP = GNI. *Rather, the problem lies in the fact that aggregate demand does not always equal GNI.* Economic instability arises because aggregate demand fluctuates relative to income.[1] As a consequence, the market for total output and the amount businessmen are willing to produce can often be either more or less than potential output.

For an explanation of the factors that determine the level of spending, causing it sometimes to fall short of potential output, we must look to the rela-

[1]There is a subtle distinction to be made here. Although a shortage of *aggregate* purchasing power cannot be the reason why market demand falls short of potential GNP (since GNP = GNI), the *distribution* of GNI can play an important role. Who gets the income helps to determine the strength of aggregate demand. Some economists have maintained, for example, that an increasing concentration of income in the hands of upper-income groups led to a shortfall in aggregate demand in the 1920s and ultimately to the collapse of the economy in 1929. But whatever the validity of this contention, the problem was not an aggregate shortage of purchasing power, but rather its maldistribution.

tions between income and aggregate demand. This is the basic task of the remainder of the chapter: an investigation of how aggregate demand is related to GNI, and how, in turn, this relationship determines the level of GNP.

The major components of aggregate demand are consumption, investment, and government purchases. We turn first to consumption spending, and in particular to the relation between consumption and income.

## THE DETERMINANTS
## OF AGGREGATE DEMAND

/ The Consumption Function /

*Family income–consumption relationships.* The consumption of individual families depends heavily on the size of their disposable income. In technical language, consumption is a *function* of (i.e., depends on) income, and the relation of consumption to income is called "the consumption function." Although there are wide variations in consumption behavior, rich families tend to spend more on consumption than poor families. High income generally leads to high consumption.

The nature of the relation between family income and family consumption in recent years is shown in Table 3–1, adapted from a survey of family spending patterns in 1950.[2] The first two columns of the table present the *consumption function* in the form of a schedule relating the level of consumption to the level of family income. The difference between income and consumption is *saving*, shown in the third column of the table. As we would expect, consumption spending increases as we move from low to high levels of income. But saving also increases. In other words, an increase in income tends to lead to an increase in both consumption and saving.

There are, of course, many factors other than income that affect consumption behavior—the number and ages of children in the family, the occupation of the family head, past income history, expectations about future income, and so on. Consequently, two families with the same income, but differing with respect to these other characteristics, will probably not spend the same amount on consumption goods. Nevertheless, on the average, wealthy families tend to spend more on consumption than poor families. And it is this general relation between income and consumption shown by the consumption function that we wish to examine here, for it occupies a central role in the analysis of what determines the level of gross national product.

The final four columns of the table relate to four important concepts for economic analysis—the *average propensities to consume* and *to save* and the

income – consumption = saving

an increase in income leads to increase in saving & consumption

factors which affect consumption

52

[2]The actual data given in the survey have been "smoothed" and expressed in round numbers in order to bring out more easily the basic relationships involved.

Table 3–1  FAMILY INCOME, CONSUMPTION, AND SAVING

| Disposable Family Income (After Taxes) | Consumption Expenditure | Saving | Average Propensity to Consume (APC) | Average Propensity to Save (APS) | Marginal Propensity to Consume (MPC) | Marginal Propensity to Save (MPS) |
|---|---|---|---|---|---|---|
| $2,000 | $2,150 | −$150 | 1.08 | −.08 | | |
| | | | | | .95 | .05 |
| 3,000 | 3,100 | − 100 | 1.03 | −.03 | | |
| | | | | | .90 | .10 |
| 4,000 | 4,000 | 0 | 1.00 | 0 | | |
| | | | | | .85 | .15 |
| 5,000 | 4,850 | 150 | .97 | .03 | | |
| | | | | | .80 | .20 |
| 6,000 | 5,650 | 350 | .94 | .06 | | |
| | | | | | .73 | .27 |
| 7,000 | 6,380 | 620 | .91 | .09 | | |
| | | | | | .67 | .33 |
| 8,000 | 7,050 | 950 | .88 | .12 | | |
| | | | | | .62 | .38 |
| 9,000 | 7,670 | 1,330 | .85 | .15 | | |
| | | | | | .51 | .49 |
| 10,000 | 8,180 | 1,820 | .82 | .18 | | |

*marginal propensities to consume* and *to save*. The average propensity to consume (APC) is simply the percentage of income consumed, the ratio of consumption to income. The average propensity to save (APS) is, similarly, the percentage of income that flows into savings. Since all income is either consumed or saved, the sum of APC and APS must always equal 1.00.[3] Thus, at an income level of $2,000, the average propensity to consume is 1.08; the average propensity to save is consequently minus .08. At incomes around $10,000, the average propensity to consume is .82, so that the average propensity to save is 1.00 minus .82, or .18.

Notice that the average propensity to save rises (and the average propensity to consume falls) as income increases. This confirms the general everyday observation that the rich save a larger percentage of their income than the poor. Indeed, at very low levels of income, saving is negative; on the average, families in the lowest income brackets spend more than they earn. Saving becomes positive—consumption is less than income—at incomes above $4,000 and increases not only absolutely, but relative to income as we move up to higher income brackets.

Whereas the average propensity to consume relates the level of consumption to the level of income, the *marginal* propensity to consume (MPC) relates *changes* in consumption to *changes* in income. The marginal propensity to consume is the ratio of the *change* in consumption to the *change* in income. It tells

[3] Let $C$ = consumption, $S$ = saving, $Y$ = income. Then $C + S = Y$, and $\frac{C}{Y} + \frac{S}{Y} = 1$.

53

what part of each dollar of income change will flow into additional consumption rather than additional saving. In Table 3–1, for example, an *increase* in income from $4,000 to $5,000 is associated with an *increase* in consumption from $4,000 to $4,850. We deduce from this that if families earning in the neighborhood of $4,000 receive an additional $1,000 in income, they will use $850, or 85 per cent of this increment, to increase their consumption; thus the MPC is .85. The marginal propensity to save (MPS) is the twin of the marginal propensity to consume. *It indicates the fraction of any change in income that will be saved.* Since an increase in income can be channeled only into consumption or saving, the sum of the two marginal propensities must equal 1.00; or the marginal propensity to save is equal to 1.00 minus the marginal propensity to consume.

The consumption function can also be shown graphically, as in Fig. 3–1. Along the horizontal axis of the graph we measure family disposable income; along the vertical axis we measure consumption per family. Each of the black dots in the graph represents one of the consumption–income combinations shown in the first two columns of Table 3–1. Point *C*, for example, is the combination: income = $6,000, consumption = $5,650. Since any point on a two-dimensional graph represents *two* numbers, such a graph can depict a function, the relation between two sets of numbers—in this case the relation between income and consumption. The line *CC* is a smooth line, drawn to come as close as possible to all the points on the graph. Notice that not all the points fall exactly on the line, but all are very close to it. The *CC* line is representative of the general relation between income and consumption at all income levels. In other words, this line depicts the entire consumption function, and any one point on the line depicts the relation between a particular level of income and the associated level of consumption.

The 45° line in Fig. 3–1 has been drawn in to make the interpretation of the graph easier. Any point on the 45° line has equal values on both axes. Point *B*, for example is $6,000 "out" on the income axis and $6,000 "up" on the consumption axis. Income is equally well measured by the distance *OD* and by the distance *OA*. Thus, we can use the distance between the horizontal axis and the 45° line to measure income. This device permits us to see the relation between consumption, income, and saving graphically. For example, at an income of $6,000, consumption is $5,650, given by the distance *CD*. Saving is the difference between income and consumption—i.e., *BC*. More generally, the distance from the *CC* line to the horizontal axis equals consumption, and the distance from the *CC* line to the 45° line equals saving. At point *Z* (an income of $4,000) consumption and income are equal; saving is zero. At this point the *CC* line intersects the 45° line, and, of course, the distance between the *CC* line and the 45° line is zero. At point *Y* (income of $2,000) consumption is greater than income, and saving is negative. Notice that we show this negative saving on the graph by measuring *down* from the *CC* line to the 45° line; when saving is positive—all points to the right of *Z*—we measure *up* from *CC* to the 45° line. Since the 45° line is a

54

shorthand device to enable us to measure income and consumption in the same direction, we shall henceforth call it the *income line*. In a diagram that contains a consumption function and a 45° income line, saving is the "wedge-shaped" difference between the consumption function and the income line (see Figs. 3–1, 3–2, and 3–3).

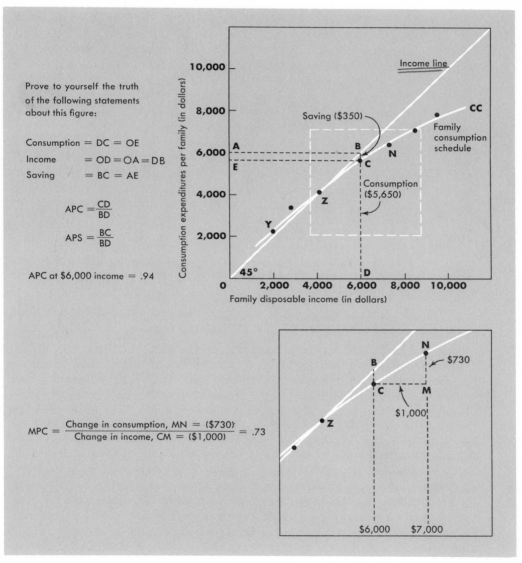

FIG. 3–1   Family consumption function

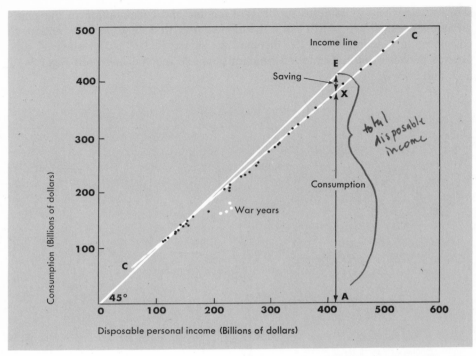

**FIG. 3–2** Disposable income-consumption relations in the United States (1929–1969). Note: both consumer expenditures and income are measured in dollars of constant purchasing power.

*National consumption–income relations.* Given the relation between income and consumption at the individual family level, total consumption expenditures for the nation as a whole tend to rise and fall with total disposable income. Figure 3–2 illustrates the national consumption function. Each dot represents the income–consumption relation of a particular year. The points representing each year's consumption and income do not fall exactly on the consumption function, but they are all very close to it, except during World War II and the immediate postwar period. The schedule *CC* thus depicts the basic relation between disposable income and consumption, although we must remember that this is only a tendency and that actual consumption may deviate moderately from this "ideal" relation. Just as in the chart of family income and consumption, the income line furnishes a shorthand way to visualize the division of income between consumption and saving. The vertical line *AE* (= *OA*) is total disposable income, which is split into consumption and saving, as shown in the figure.

As total disposable income rises, consumption rises. But just as among individual families, not all the increase in income goes toward raising consumption levels; some of it finds its way into saving. For the economy as a whole, the

56

marginal propensity to consume is, therefore, less than 1; the marginal propensity to save is positive.

### Some Other Aspects of the Consumption Function

Although consumption expenditures do rise and fall with disposable income, the behavior of consumers is more complicated than it appears from Figs. 3–1 and 3–2.

In the first place, the proportion of a family's income that is consumed is likely to depend on its income *relative* to other people's average income rather than on the absolute level of its income. In Table 3–1 and Fig. 3–1 we see, for example, that a typical family earning $4,000 in 1950 consumed all its income. In 1950, a $4,000 family income was about average. Fifty years earlier, however, a family earning $4,000 a year was well up in the income distribution and typically saved a significant fraction of its income. Today the average family income is nearly $8,000, and the "break-even" income level has risen correspondingly. "Keeping up with the Joneses" is an important feature of consumer behavior. As the general level of income rises, any *fixed* level of absolute income becomes lower relative to the average. The pressures to keep up with the rising general standard of living raise the fraction of income consumed in each absolute income bracket. Were we to draw Fig. 3–1 for the year 1900, the consumption schedule would be far lower and would cross the 45° line (where consumption equals income) at a much lower level than in 1950; the consumption function for 1980 would be much higher. Thus, just because at any one moment of time higher family incomes are associated with a higher average propensity to save, we cannot conclude that the average propensity to save for the nation as a whole will also rise in response to the gradual rise in income. As a matter of fact, over the past hundred years, despite a sixfold rise in average family income, the fraction of income saved has not risen.

Another feature of consumer behavior with important implications for economic stability is that in the short run *consumer purchases generally do not fluctuate as sharply as income*. Consumers tend to adjust their consumption habits to their longer-term income prospects. A wage earner who suddenly becomes unemployed or a small businessman who has a bad year will normally not expect his income to remain at that low level, and will tend, for a while at least, to maintain consumption at its earlier level. Should it turn out that his income remains low for a long period, then he will have to gradually adjust his consumption; but, temporarily at least, he tries to preserve most of his accustomed living standard. One of the reasons why consumption in the lower-income groups exceeds income (see Fig. 3–1) is that many families are only temporarily poor. Their consumption is affected by the fact that they do not expect to remain at the low income level and by the living standards to which they had become accustomed. For these same reasons, consumption expenditures for the nation as a whole at the trough of the Great Depression were slightly higher than disposable income (see Fig. 3–2).

However complicated the relations underlying the consumption function, consumption does tend to rise and fall as income rises and falls. Even more important is the fact that the change in consumption is less, in absolute amount, than the change in income—*the marginal propensity to consume is less than 1.*

### HOW GNP IS DETERMINED:
### A SIMPLIFIED EXAMPLE

Our central problem is to determine the relations between production, incomes, and spending. And to solve the problem realistically we will need to consider the full range of interconnections portrayed rather fearsomely in Fig. 2–5 in the last chapter—including the production, income, and spending relations for households, businesses, and government—and all at the same time!

But to begin, to get at the essentials, let us look at a rather simpler world. Let us suppose that all saving is done by households—no gross business saving at all! And let us assume that there is no government (and that the rest of the world does not exist). Then all GNI goes to disposable income; neither taxes nor business saving exists. And there are only two kinds of spending—consumption and business investment. In this simple case aggregate demand, which determines the level of GNP, will depend solely on just two elements: the consumption function of households and the investment decisions of business.

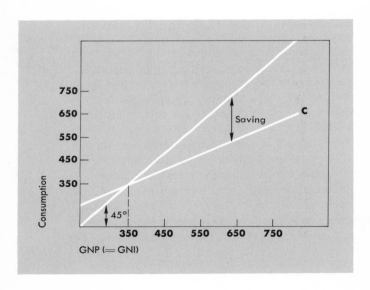

**FIG. 3–3** Consumption function

Suppose that business has decided to invest $80 billion and that this level stays unchanged no matter what the level of GNP. Also suppose that the consumption function is of the form shown in Fig. 3–3. These two facts can be put together in a new diagram, Fig. 3–4, which plots total spending (this figure is a more formal, graphic presentation of the circular flow diagram).

The line C + I in Fig. 3–4 is, of course, the sum of the consumption function and investment. The consumption function tells us how much will be spent on consumption at each possible level of GNI. We have temporarily assumed that investment is constant (at $80 billion in this case) and does not change as GNP and GNI change. Clearly, then, if we add the (constant) level of investment to the consumption function, the result tells us the level of aggregate spending that would be forthcoming at each possible level of GNP and GNI.

*The line C + I, therefore, is the aggregate demand schedule indicating the level of total spending that would occur at each possible level of GNP (= GNI).*

} * C+I = aggregate demand

Out of all the possible levels of GNP, however, only one level will actually tend to be produced. And that level will be the one at which production (GNP) is matched by total spending (aggregate demand). If business is not to pile up

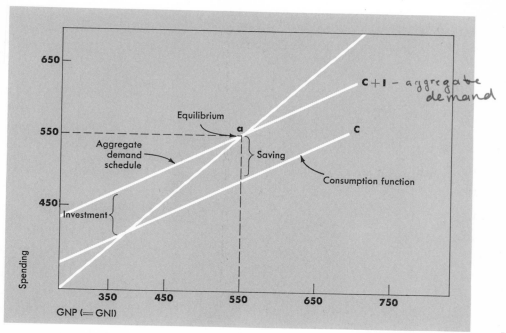

FIG. 3–4  Aggregate demand

unwanted inventories, total spending must equal total production. In Fig. 3–4 that occurs at point *a*, where aggregate demand (*C* + *I*) just equals GNP, with both equal to 550. This is the *equilibrium* level of GNP, where spending matches production.

*The equilibrium level of GNP, the level that will tend to be produced, is that level at which aggregate demand just matches GNP. In diagram form this is the point at which the aggregate demand schedule (C + I) intersects the 45° income line.*

Suppose GNP does not equal 550, but is, say, 650 (see Fig. 3–5). Then aggregate demand will be 610, and 40 units will remain unsold. Production will then be contracted or cut back until it matches demand, which will be at 550.

What if production is only 450? Then total aggregate demand will be 490; part of the demand will have to be met out of inventories; and business will expand production, thus raising income and demand, until equilibrium between production and aggregate demand is again reached at 550.

Notice that at the equilibrium point two conditions occur:

- aggregate demand equals GNP
- saving equals investment

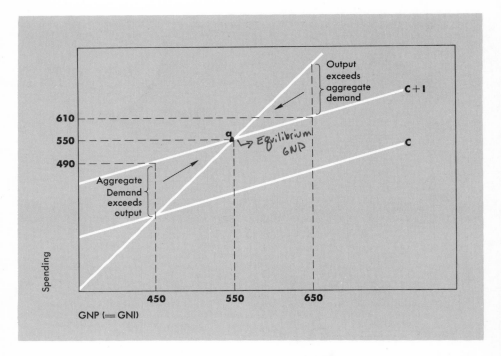

FIG. 3–5 Determination of equilibrium GNP

60

This is the nub of the solution. Business firms will tend to produce that level of output which is matched by total spending. The production of output will, as we have continually repeated, give rise to an equal amount of income. Some of the income will be spent on consumption; the rest is saved. When GNP is at that level where saving is exactly matched by investment, then it is also at a level where spending equals output. This is the equilibrium level of the GNP; the one level out of all possible levels toward which production will tend. Saving is the unspent leakage out of income; investment spending must match that leakage to balance production and spending. To put this another way, in order for a particular level of GNP and GNI to be the equilibrium level, that part of GNI which is *not* spent on consumption (i.e., saving) must be spent on something else (i.e., investment). If at some particular level of GNP and GNI saving tends to exceed investment, then total spending is too low to sustain that level of GNP and GNP will fall. If, on the other hand, investment tends to exceed saving, total spending is too high for that particular level of GNP and GNP will rise.

*GNP & GNI in relation to spending*

This point can be illustrated more directly by Fig. 3–6. It shows how saving is related to income. (See if you can derive this curve from Fig. 3–3.) Saving turns positive at $350 billion and continues to rise with higher incomes. Investment is given equal to $80 billion. At only one income level, where GNP and GNI equal $550 billion, does saving equal investment.

Notice that this process does not assure full use of potential: *the equilibrium GNP need not be the same as full-employment GNP.* In this simple case, equilibrium GNP depends solely on investment demand and the consumption function. Even in more sophisticated cases we take up later, the basic conclusion remains. The essential reason is this: the decision to save is in the hands of consumers. The decision to invest is in the hands of business firms. The equilibrium level of GNP will be that level which equates total saving with total investment—the only level at which aggregate demand equals total production and income. It would

*equilibrium GNP not always = full employment GNP*

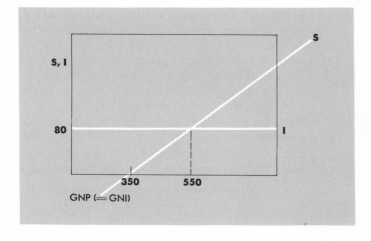

**FIG. 3–6** Equilibrium of saving and investment

be sheer accident if these decisions were such as to produce precise equality of saving and investment at full-employment GNP. If the saving forthcoming at full-employment levels of GNP exceeds investment, then full-employment GNP will not be reached. The output of a fully employed economy cannot be sold. Conversely if investment exceeds saving at full-employment GNI, then aggregate demand will exceed potential GNP and there will be inflation.

Given the consumption function, achieving and sustaining full employment requires matching the volume of saving that would be forthcoming from a fully employed economy with an equal volume of investment demand. In short, that portion of income generated by a full-employment economy which would not be spent on consumption goods must be spent on other goods if full-employment production is actually to be achieved.

### An Arithmetic Presentation[4]

The determination of equilibrium GNP can also be shown by numerical illustration. The first column in Table 3–2 lists various possible levels of GNP (= GNI). The second column gives the volume of purchases that consumers would make at each level of GNI. The difference between column 1 and column 2 is saving, the amount of total GNI not spent on consumption goods (shown in column 3).

As a first approximation, we assume that the level of investment demand is fixed at $80 billion and does not vary as GNP changes. It is shown in column 4. Adding columns 2 and 4 gives the total volume of aggregate demand—i.e., the sum of consumption and investment, shown in column 5. At each possible level of total output there would occur, therefore, a particular level of aggregate demand, given by the consumption function on the one hand and investment spending on the other. Column 5 is, in effect, a *schedule of aggregate demand*, showing the total spending on goods and services that would be made at each possible level of GNI. Column 6, in turn, gives the difference between aggregate demand and total output. At low levels of GNP, demand would tend to exceed output; at high levels, output would exceed demand. But business firms will tend to produce that level of output which can find a market. In Table 3–2 there is only one such output—$550 billion. Any other level of output would either exceed or fall short of aggregate demand. Column 7 shows the excess of investment over saving. It is exactly the same as the excess of demand over output (plus or minus). Only at a GNP of $550 billion does investment equal saving, and it is at this GNP that aggregate demand equals output.

Consider the first row in Table 3–2, where GNP is $400 billion. At this level, production would fall short of aggregate demand by $60 billion. Clearly, therefore, this is not the level of GNP that would be produced. Higher levels of GNP would be accompanied by higher sales; but the increase in sales would be less than the increase in GNP, because the marginal propensity to consume is

[4]An algebraic presentation is given in the Appendix to this chapter.

Table 3–2   THE "EQUILIBRIUM" LEVEL OF GNP

(Billions of Dollars)

| GNP = GNI 1 | Consumption 2 | Saving 3 | Investment 4 | Aggregate Demand (2 + 4) 5 | Aggregate Demand Minus Output (5 — 1) 6 | Investment Minus Saving (4 — 3) 7 | |
|---|---|---|---|---|---|---|---|
| 400 | 380 | 20 | 80 | 460 | 60 | 60 | Demand |
| 450 | 410 | 40 | 80 | 490 | 40 | 40 | Exceeds |
| 500 | 440 | 60 | 80 | 520 | 20 | 20 | Output |
| 550 | 470 | 80 | 80 | 550 | 0 | 0 | Equilibrium |
| 600 | 500 | 100 | 80 | 580 | —20 | —20 | Output |
| 650 | 530 | 120 | 80 | 610 | —40 | —40 | Exceeds Demand |

less than 1; some of the additional GNI would flow into savings and only the remainder into added consumption expenditures. A rise in GNP from $400 billion to $500 billion would be accompanied by a rise in consumption from $380 to $440 billion; the marginal propensity to consume is .6 ($60 billion added consumption out of $100 million added GNP). At this level of GNP the excess of demand over output would have been reduced to $20 billion. But only at a GNP of $550 billion will the excess be eliminated. Levels of output higher than $550 billion would lead to a situation in which demand was less than output; sales would not be sufficient to take off the market all the goods produced.

GNP will thus tend to be established at that level where aggregate demand equals output. Aggregate demand, in turn, will equal output when that part of GNI that is *not* spent on consumption goods *is* spent on investment. And as column 7 shows, saving is matched by investment demand only at a $550 billion level of GNP. Only at that level of GNP is the gap between total output and consumption spending exactly equal to investment.

## GROSS BUSINESS SAVING
## AND THE DETERMINATION OF GNP

So much for the case of the simple circular flow with just one form of leakage—personal saving. That case had the singular advantage that GNI and disposable income were the same thing: neither business nor government absorbed income. But we saw in Chapter 2 that disposable personal income accounts for only part of total gross national income. The rest goes to business firms as retained earnings and depreciation, which we have called *gross business saving*, and to government in the form of *tax revenues*. For the moment, however, let

*gross business saving*

*tax revenue*

us add only one complication at a time. We will continue to assume an economy with no government and no taxes. But let us now take *gross business saving* into account. Business firms do not pay out in dividends all their profits and depreciation. They retain some of these funds in the business. Hence gross national income is composed of two elements: gross business saving and disposable personal income.

As GNP (= GNI) increases, business profits also tend to rise by a roughly predictable amount. Profits, after all, are closely related to the level of business activity. Out of profits a portion is paid to stockholders in dividends and the remainder is retained in the business. Consequently, for each level of GNI there exists a corresponding level of gross business saving that does not flow into disposable income, but as its name implies, is retained by business.

Out of each dollar of additional income generated by an increase in GNP, therefore, part flows into gross business saving and the remainder goes to disposable personal income. Out of any increase in disposable income, in turn, the consumption function tells us what part is saved by individuals and what part is consumed. An example will be useful:

Suppose GNI (= GNP) increases by ............................................... $1.00

    a. As much as 40¢ might go to gross business profits. But of that 40¢ some 15¢ may be paid out in dividends and therefore flow into disposable income. The remaining 25¢ remains with business as gross business saving ................................................................. .25

    b. Disposable personal income will rise by $1.00 *less* the 25¢ flowing into gross business saving ............................................ .75

    c. Consumption will not rise by the full amount of the 75¢ increase in disposable personal income; some of it will be saved. If the marginal propensity to consume out of disposable income is .80, then consumption will rise by (.80 × .75) .......................... .60

In view of these relationships, we can say that consumption is tied to GNP by a two-link chain:

- For every GNP (= GNI) there is an associated level of disposable personal income.
- For every level of disposable personal income there is an associated level of consumption spending.

When GNP changes, consumption will also change in an amount determined by the combination of these two relationships. But the change in consumption is normally significantly less than the change in GNP.

The change in consumption associated with a change in disposable income we have called the marginal propensity to consume, MPC. Let us call the change in consumption associated with the change in GNP the *consumption–GNP relation* and denote its marginal value by *MPC_g*.

The consumption–GNP relation is shown in Fig. 3–7. The dotted line shows how disposable income rises as GNP and GNI rise. The wedge-shaped gap between the disposable income line and the 45° income line measures gross business saving; i.e., gross business saving is the difference between GNI and disposable income, a gap that rises as GNI rises. Similarly, the wedge-shaped gap between the consumption function and the disposable income line is personal saving. The production of a gross national product equal to *OK* (or *EK*) would be accompanied by the generation of an equal amount of gross national income, leading to gross business saving of *EG* and personal disposable income of *GK*. Out of this disposable income, *FK* would be consumed. The remainder, *EF*, represents the amount of total income that is not consumed; it is equal to gross business saving *EG* plus personal saving *FG*.

*OK* is the equilibrium GNP; investment must be equal to *EG* + *FG*, the sum of gross business and personal saving. And to achieve a *full-employment equilibrium*, investment must equal the amount of gross business and personal saving that would issue from full-employment GNP. The basic rules for the determination of GNP are unchanged. That level of GNP will tend to be produced where aggregate demand equals output, where the amount not spent on consump-

*full employment equilibrium*

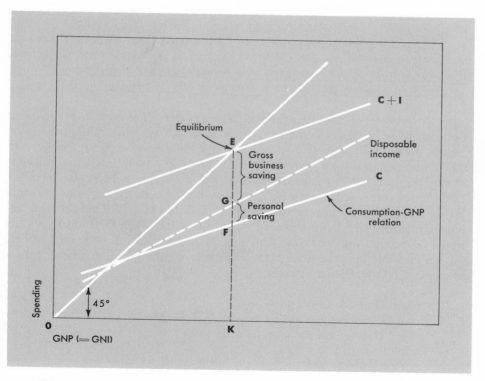

FIG. 3–7 The consumption-GNP relation, gross business saving, and equilibrium GNP

tion (saving) is just offset by an equal amount spent on investment. The only difference between this and the simpler model presented earlier is that total saving now includes gross business saving as well as personal saving. Since there is more saving, a smaller part of GNI is spent on consumption goods. Investment must therefore be larger in order to match the higher saving and equate aggregate demand with output.

## GOVERNMENT SPENDING AND
## TAXATION IN THE EQUILIBRIUM GNP

So far we have ignored the role of government in the determination of GNP. We must now expand our model of the process by which the level of GNP is established to incorporate the influence of government taxation and spending. Two modifications of our earlier model are required: first, we must take account, in calculating the consumption–GNP relation, that part of total GNI that "leaks" off into taxes; and second, we must include government purchases of goods and services as part of total aggregate demand.

| Taxes |

Up to this point in the chapter we have assumed that total GNI was split into just two components, gross business saving and disposable personal income. *We must now recognize that disposable personal income is less than GNI not only by the amount of gross business saving but also by the amount of taxes paid to government.*

Government tax revenues rise and fall with GNP, since most taxes are based on personal or business income or on sales volume. Given the nation's tax laws, we can predict fairly closely how tax revenues will change as GNP changes. As GNP increases, therefore, part of the additional GNI flows into gross business saving, *part into government tax revenues*, and the rest into disposable income.[5] In turn, that increase in disposable income is divided between increased personal saving and increased consumption. Adding taxes to our model means that disposable income, and hence consumption, changes less when GNP changes than would be the case without taxes. With a modification of the example used earlier, we can illustrate how the $MPC_g$ (the change in consumption associated with a change in GNI) is affected by taxes.

Suppose GNI (= GNP) increases by ............................................... $1.00
    a.   Gross business saving may increase by 25¢ ......................... .25
    b.   *Government tax revenues will rise* by 20¢ ............................ .20

[5]Government transfer payments offset part of the effect of taxes. We treat them as negative taxes and use net taxes in the illustrations.

c. Disposable personal income will rise by $1.00, *less* the amount of the increased income flowing to gross business saving (25¢) and *taxes* (20¢). Disposable personal income will therefore rise by (1.00 − .25 − .20) ............................................................................ .55

d. Consumption will not rise by the full amount of the rise in disposable personal income. If the marginal propensity to consume out of disposable income is .80, then consumption will rise by (.80 × .55) ............................................................................ .44

Thus the consumption–GNP relation is changed when we add to our model the effects of government taxes. Part of the rise in GNI is now absorbed by increased taxes, leading to a smaller increase in disposable income and, therefore, in consumption. Line *C* in Fig. 3–7 is lowered (because consumption at any level of GNP is less) and is flatter (because consumption changes less when GNP changes).

### Government Purchases

Although the imposition of taxes tends to lower consumption spending and therefore aggregate demand, government purchases of goods and services increase aggregate demand. We must now think of aggregate demand as being composed of three elements—consumption, investment, and government purchases of goods and services. GNP will therefore tend to be established at that level where output is matched by the sum of consumption, investment, and government spending. Aggregate demand will equal total output when that part of income *not* spent on consumption (business saving, personal saving, and taxes) is matched by the sum of investment and government spending; or, more briefly, when total saving plus taxes is equaled by investment plus government spending.

How GNP is determined when we include government in our calculation is shown in Fig. 3–8. The *C* line reflects the new consumption–GNP relation, and is drawn to take into account the fact that some of GNI "leaks" off into taxes as well as into business and personal saving. It is lower and has a flatter slope than the line *C* in Fig. 3–7. To indicate the level of total aggregate demand, we add government purchases *G* to the *C* + *I* line. The schedule of aggregate demand is now given by the line labeled *C* + *I* + *G*. At the equilibrium level of GNP, output and aggregate demand are equal, and this is the level to which GNP will tend to gravitate. At this point, the portion of GNI *not* spent on consumption goods (business saving plus personal saving plus taxes) is matched by *I* + *G*, investors' and government spending.

## THE MULTIPLIER

So far we have discussed the determination of the equilibrium level of GNP for given amounts of investment and government spending. What if

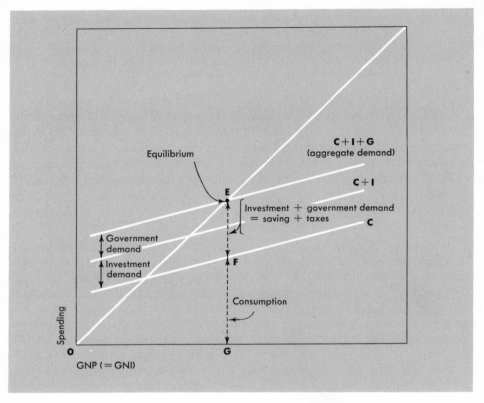

**FIG. 3–8** The equilibrium level of GNP (government included)

investment or government spending increases? It is, of course, clear that a change in investment and government spending will lead to a change in GNP in the same direction. With the aid of Fig. 3–8 or Table 3–2 we can see that a given change in $I + G$ will result in a change in GNP *greater* than the initial change in $I + G$. Look back at Table 3–2. There we assumed that the level of investment demand was $80 billion; equilibrium GNP, in that case, was $550 billion. Suppose that investment rose to $100 billion. GNP would rise, not just by $20 billion, but by $50 billion, to a new level of $600 billion. At this new level of total output and income, consumption spending would be $500 billion. With investment spending equal to $100 billion, aggregate demand would be $600 billion, precisely equal to the total value of output. Thus, an initial rise of $20 billion in spending by investors would ultimately lead to a rise of $50 billion in aggregate demand and therefore would induce a similar rise of $50 billion in GNP.

The reason for this multiple impact on GNP of a rise in investment (or government) spending is to be found in the fact *that <u>when total income rises, consumption spending also rises.</u>* Based on the consumption–GNP relation, $MPC_g$ is less than 1 but greater than zero. As a consequence, when an initial increase in aggregate demand leads to a rise in output and income, still further increases in aggregate demand are thereby set in motion, since the initial rise in income is followed by increases in consumer spending. In the situation we have depicted, business firms are assumed to increase their purchases of plant and equipment by $20 billion. Construction firms and firms producing machinery find their orders and sales rising. They therefore increase their output by $20 billion to meet this new demand. Their increase in output generates an additional $20 billion of income, chiefly in the form of higher wages and larger profits. In turn, this increase in income induces a secondary rise in consumption spending. Assume, for example, that the $MPC_g$ is .6. Then the $20 billion of extra income from the production of additional investment (or government) goods would raise consumer spending by $12 billion. Production of consumer goods now increases, with a further $12 billion increase in income. This leads to still another rise in consumer spending (by .6 × $12 billion, or $7.2 billion). And so the process continues.

Thus an initial advance in spending and output gives rise to a "chain effect." Higher spending leads to higher output, which, in turn, raises incomes and gives a further impetus to new consumer spending. Notice, however, that the successive increases in spending and income are smaller at each stage of the process. Since not all the extra GNI reaches households and part of the extra disposable income is saved, only part of each increment to income is re-spent. The ultimate rise in GNP is limited as the increments to spending grow successively smaller.

The specific impact of a change in investment or government spending on the size of GNP can be calculated in the following way. (The symbol $\Delta$ in the calculation means "change in"; thus $\Delta I$ means "change in investment spending.")

1. Assume a change in investment spending, $\Delta I$, of $20 billion. There will be an initial rise of income generated by the production of this additional plant and equipment. The additional income—equal to the additional output of plant and equipment—will be:

$$\Delta I = 20$$

2. Assume the $MPC_g$ is .6 ($\Delta C = .6 \, \Delta GNP$). The *initial* change in income will then give rise to a change in consumption spending and a consequent secondary increase in output and income of:

$$.6 \times 20 = 12$$

3. In turn, this *second* increase in income will result in still further consumer spending equal to:

*how to calculate effect on GNP of change in investment spending*

69

$$.6 \times .6 \times 20 = .36(20) = 7.2$$

4. This process will continue, as a fraction of each additional increase in income is spent on consumer goods, which, in turn, induces consumer-goods firms to increase output and income still further. The total increase in GNP will, of course, be equal to the sum of all these increments:

| | |
|---|---|
| $\Delta$GNP $= 20$ | (initial change in spending and output) |
| $+ .6(20)$ | $(= 12$   or a total of 32   by the second round) |
| $+ .36(20)$ | $(= 7.2 \;''\; '' \;\;\; '' \;\;\; '' \; 39.6 \;'' \;\; '' \;\;$ third $\;\;\;\;\; '' \;\;\; )$ |
| $+ .22(20)$ | $(= 4.4 \;'' \; '' \;\;\; '' \;\;\; '' \; 43.6 \;'' \;\; '' \;\;$ fourth $\;\;\; '' \;\;\; )$ |
| $+ .14(20)$ | $(= 2.8 \;'' \; '' \;\;\; '' \;\;\; '' \; 46.4 \;'' \;\; '' \;\;$ fifth $\;\;\;\;\; '' \;\;\; )$ |
| $+ .08(20)$ | $(= 1.6 \;'' \; '' \;\;\; '' \;\;\; '' \; 48.0 \;'' \;\; '' \;\;$ sixth $\;\;\;\;\; '' \;\;\; )$ |
| etc. | etc. |

                                                        $\overline{50}$

$\Delta$GNP $= 50$        (increase in equilibrium GNP)

5. From the formula for a geometric series we know that as the number of links in the chain is extended indefinitely this sum, and therefore the total rise in GNP, will equal:

$$\Delta\text{GNP} = \frac{1}{(1 - .6)}\, 20 = \frac{1}{.4}\,(20) = (2\tfrac{1}{2})\, 20 = 50$$

More generally, $\Delta\text{GNP} = \dfrac{1}{1 - \text{MPC}_g}\, \Delta I$

Thus the ultimate change in GNP will be a multiple of the initial change in spending. *The ratio that shows the ultimate change in GNP resulting from an initial change in spending is called the multiplier.*

As can be seen from the above example, we can write the multiplier as

$$\frac{1}{1 - \text{MPC}_g}$$

We can also define $\text{MPS}_g$ to be the marginal propensity to save out of GNI, again including net taxes and business and personal saving. (Or to be more precise, we could simply call it the marginal propensity *not* to spend!) Then:

$$\text{MPC}_g + \text{MPS}_g = 1, \quad \text{or } \text{MPS}_g = 1 - \text{MPC}_g$$

and the multiplier becomes simply the reciprocal of the marginal propensity to save out of GNI,

$$\text{multiplier} = \frac{1}{\text{MPS}_g}$$

In the example worked out above, the multiplier is 2½. The larger the multiplier, the greater the response of total output and income to initial changes in investment and government spending. The size of the multiplier itself depends on the magnitude of $\text{MPC}_g$. This algebraic result only confirms common sense. If $\text{MPC}_g$ is close to 1, then almost all of any new increment to income will be re-spent on consumer goods and the chain effect of income → spending → income will not quickly taper off. The multiplier will be quite large. Conversely, if $\text{MPC}_g$ is small—because large fractions of additions to income are absorbed by savings and taxes—the initial change in income will result in only small additional changes in consumer spending; the resultant chain effect will rapidly diminish, and the ultimate change in GNP will be modest. The multiplier, in this case, will be small. It should be clear, of course, that the multiplier workers both ways. An initial *reduction* in spending results in a multiplied reduction in GNP.

How an initial change in spending leads to a new equilibrium level of GNP can be seen in Fig. 3–9. Diagram I shows the equilibrium GNP ($550 billion) at point $E$, where aggregate demand equals output. Suppose investment now increases by $20 billion, as shown in diagram II. The new aggregate demand schedule shifts upward. With a multiplier of 2½, a $20 billion rise in investment spending leads to a $50 billion rise in GNP. At the new equilibrium $E'$, aggregate demand has risen by $50 billion; investment demand rose $20 billion, and the induced rise in consumer spending was $30 billion. (With a $\text{MPC}_g$ of .6, the $50 billion rise in GNI induced a $30 billion rise in consumption.) A decrease in investment spending would have similar results in the opposite direction.

*Any* initial change in spending can set off a multiplier impact. All our examples so far have related to a change in investment spending. But a change in government purchases has exactly the same multiplier impact. An increase in government purchases, with tax rates held constant, shifts upward the aggregate demand schedule and results in a new equilibrium GNP; as in the case of an increase in investment spending, the rise in GNP will be larger than the rise in government spending that initiated the multiplier chain effect. In Fig. 3–9, a $20 billion rise in government purchases could be substituted for the $20 billion rise in investment, and the over-all results, in terms of GNP, would be the same.

In a similar manner, a shift upward in the consumption function—i.e., more is consumed out of each dollar of disposable income—would also raise the aggregate demand schedule and lead to a multiplied increase in GNP. In the summer of 1950, for example, when the Korean war began, consumers were fearful that

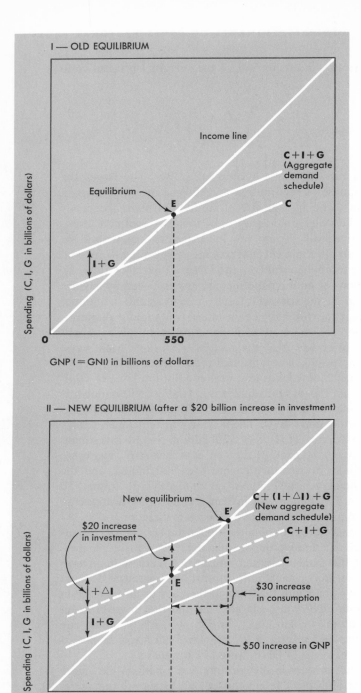

FIG. 3–9 The multiplier in diagram form

prices would rise and that rationing would be imposed. As a result, they went on a buying splurge. The consumption function temporarily shifted upward very sharply, and a large increase in GNP occurred well before government expenditures for military equipment had actually increased. These shifts set off a multiplier process.

In short, *any initial change in spending* by government, business, or consumers will tend to change the aggregate demand schedule and, through the multiplier chain effect, will lead to a change in GNP larger than the initial change in spending. The size of the multiplier depends on the size of $MPC_g$; the larger the share of any change in GNI that flows into consumption spending, the larger the multiplier.

### Changes In Taxes

An increase in government spending *raises* the aggregate demand schedule and therefore increases GNP; an increase in taxes *reduces* purchases by private individuals and firms, thus *lowering* the aggregate demand schedule and GNP. Taxes channel income from private individuals and business firms to the government. They consequently reduce private purchasing power and spending and free resources for the production of goods and services for the government. The higher government tax rates are, the larger is the proportion of total GNI that flows to government, and the smaller is the proportion flowing to consumers. (Taxes on corporate profits also affect retained business earnings and investment, but in this chapter we shall not pursue this point.) Lower consumer incomes mean lower consumption purchases. When taxes are increased, therefore, the volume of consumption purchases out of any given GNP will be lower—in other words, *the consumption–GNP relation will shift downward as taxes are increased and shift upward as taxes are decreased*.

The effect of changes in tax rates on consumption is shown in Fig. 3–10. $C_1$ is the consumption–GNP relation indicating what consumption purchases will be at each level of GNP (= GNI). It takes into account the fraction of gross national income that is absorbed by business saving and taxes and is therefore unavailable for consumption spending. Suppose, for example, that tax rates are such that when GNP is at $500 billion, the government collects $120 billion in net taxes; let us also suppose that $60 billion of total GNI goes to gross business saving, resulting in a disposable income of $320 billion. Suppose consumption is $280 billion.

| | | |
|---:|:-:|---:|
| GNP (= GNI) | : | $500 |
| *less* taxes | : | 120 |
| *less* gross business saving | : | 60 |
| disposable income | : | 320 |
| consumption | : | 280 |

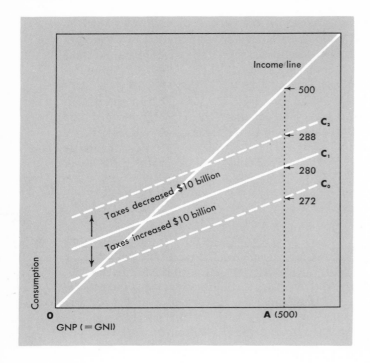

FIG. 3–10 How changes in taxes affect the consumption-GNP relation

Now assume that the government raises tax rates in order to collect an additional $10 billion out of the same $500 billion GNP. In that case the consumption–GNP relation will decline to $C_0$ in Fig. 3–10. Out of the $500 billion GNI, the government would now be collecting $10 billion more; consumers would have $10 billion less in disposable income. In turn, assuming MPC to be equal to .80, consumption would be $8 billion lower. Under the old tax system, $280 billion was consumed out of the $500 billion GNI. With the new and higher tax level, $272 billion is consumed out of the $500 billion GNI:

| | | |
|---|---|---|
| GNP (= GNI) | : | $500 |
| *less* taxes | : | 130 |
| *less* gross business saving | : | 60 |
| disposable income | : | 310 |
| consumption | : | 272 |

Thus, an increase in taxes on personal income lowers the fraction of GNI that is consumed; such a tax increase reduces disposable income and lowers the consumption–GNP relation. The system is now out of equilibrium. Through the working of the multiplier a new, lower GNP equilibrium will be reached.

Conversely, a *reduction in taxes* raises the share of GNI consumed and

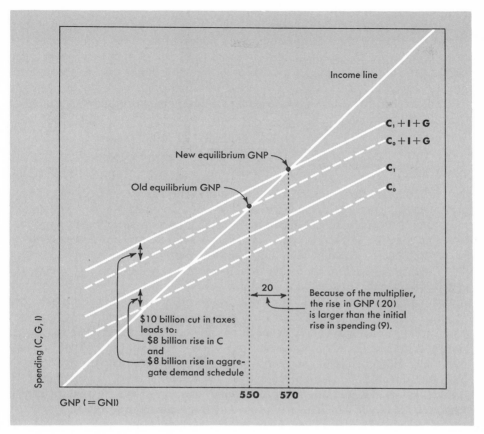

Income line

$C_1 + I + G$

$C_0 + I + G$

$C_1$

$C_0$

New equilibrium GNP

Old equilibrium GNP

20

Because of the multiplier, the rise in GNP (20) is larger than the initial rise in spending (9).

$10 billion cut in taxes leads to:
$8 billion rise in C and
$8 billion rise in aggregate demand schedule

Spending (C, G, I)

GNP (= GNI)

550   570

**FIG. 3–11**   A cut in taxes leads to a rise in GNP.

thereby *raises the consumption–GNP relation*. This increase raises GNP, as Fig. 3–11 shows. When the consumption line shifts upward because of the tax reduction, the aggregate demand schedule also shifts upward. And, because of the multiplier, the ultimate increase in GNP is larger than the initial increase in consumer spending. With a multiplier of 2½, the $8 billion upward shift in consumption would lead to a $20 billion increase in GNP.

Changes in taxes, of course, need not fall solely on personal income. Corporate profits taxes, for example, may be raised or lowered. Here the principal impact on the economy comes through the effect that such tax changes may have on business investment. A reduction in corporate profits taxes will tend to raise investment, the aggregate demand schedule, and therefore GNP. An increase in corporate profits taxes, conversely, will depress investment and GNP.

## GOVERNMENT FISCAL POLICY[6]

Fiscal policy is government's attempt to vary its expenditures and taxes to influence the over-all level of GNP. The basic principles of government fiscal policy are quite straightforward, even though it is not easy to forecast the precise magnitude or timing of the results. During a period of unemployment when demand is too low relative to potential GNP, the government can increase demand in two ways:

1. By an *increase in government spending.*
2. By a *decrease in taxes.*

In both cases the multiplier will make the ultimate rise in GNP larger than the initial change in government spending or taxes. In effect, the government can raise total aggregate demand either by increasing its own spending or by stimulating an increase in private spending through a tax reduction. Either route to full employment (or a combination of the two) is feasible.

The use of fiscal policy for the attainment of full employment is a relatively new development. Up until the 1930s, it was standard doctrine that the most appropriate policy for the federal government during a depression was a balanced budget. In 1932 Franklin D. Roosevelt campaigned on this platform. Far from being willing to incur a budget deficit by raising expenditures or reducing taxes, most government leaders espoused exactly the opposite policy. Just a few years ago it was still considered risky for a politician openly to avow the principle of deliberately incurring a temporary budget deficit during an economic recession. Gradually, however, the belief that fiscal policy can and should be used to achieve economic stability at a high level of prosperity has come to be accepted.

The fact that expenditure increases or tax reductions can stimulate GNP does not mean that these policies can be pursued without limit. When actual GNP is below potential, a fiscal policy aimed at increasing total spending can raise the level of real output. But when GNP is already at its potential, further expansion of output is limited by the growth of potential, and additional increases in spending will simply lead to inflation. Indeed, when aggregate demand exceeds or threatens to exceed potential GNP—when, in other words, the nation is seeking to purchase a greater amount of output than it can produce—fiscal policy should aim at *decreasing* aggregate demand. Reductions in government spending or increases in taxes are called for to head off the threatened inflation.

*The object of fiscal policy is to keep actual output close to potential without overreaching that potential.* This implies a fiscal policy designed at times to stimulate total spending in the economy (when actual GNP is less than potential) and

[6]A comprehensive discussion of government fiscal policy is given in *Public Finance*, 2nd ed., by Otto Eckstein, another volume in this Series.

at other times designed to restrict excessive spending (when actual spending threatens to overrun the potential).

### Problems in the Use of Fiscal Policy

Although the basic fundamentals are straightforward enough, there are numerous conceptual and practical problems involved in achieving an ideal fiscal policy. Our tax system is a complicated structure, and an increase or decrease in taxes can be accomplished in a number of different ways. The kind of changes that are appropriate under a particular set of circumstances is not a question on which agreement is easy to reach. Fiscal policy measures take time to exert their effect on the economy. Unfortunately, those time lags are difficult to estimate and seem to vary in length in differing situations. When inflationary expectations have taken hold, so that consumers and businessmen confidently expect sales and prices to keep rising, it may take some time for fiscal policy to "bite." The reduction in disposable income resulting from a tax increase may not immediately restrain spending. Our knowledge of exactly how and when changes in taxes and government expenditures affect aggregate demand is far from perfect. As a consequence, we are not able, through fiscal and monetary policy, to keep actual GNP precisely in line with potential GNP. Nevertheless, we have come a long way from the period prior to World War II, when the economy was at the mercy of erratic swings in aggregate demand. Even if perfection is far from our grasp, we do know how to moderate swings in GNP; we can take action to moderate inflationary surges and reverse incipient economic recessions.

In evaluating fiscal policy, it is important to remember that we can never actually observe its results. Imagine a situation in which aggregate demand begins collapsing. Business firms, home buyers, and purchasers of consumer durables start to reduce their spending. Let us assume that, left unchecked, GNP would decline sufficiently below potential that unemployment would rise from 4 to 8 per cent of the labor force. Now assume that the federal government steps in with a series of fiscal policy measures—tax cuts and spending increases—that successfully offsets three fourths of the GNP decline. Unemployment rises not to 8 per cent but only to 5 per cent. Simply observing the facts, a superficial critic might complain that fiscal policy was ineffective. A recession did occur; unemployment did rise, despite the fiscal actions. But in reality, fiscal policy was effective in this situation. One might legitimately criticize the government for failing to realize the full extent of the impending recession and for offering too small a fiscal package. But it would not be legitimate to argue that the rise of unemployment in the face of fiscal policy actions showed that countercyclical fiscal policy was worthless. In judging economic policy, we have to measure results against "what might otherwise have occurred."

A fuller exposition of fiscal policy, both its strengths and the difficulties associated with it, may be found in the *Public Finance* volume of this Series. The

*Money and Credit* volume of the Series discusses the relationship of monetary and fiscal policy.

*[handwritten: monetary policy]*

Fiscal policy is not the only tool available to the government for pursuing the objective of a stable economy. The government also makes use of *monetary policy.* The government can influence the supply of money (currency and checking accounts) in the hands of the public. It can thereby affect credit conditions— the interest rates borrowers must pay and the ease with which they can secure loans. The means by which the government affects the money supply and credit conditions are explained in the *Money and Credit: Impact and Control* volume of this Series. At this juncture the major point to remember is that when the supply of money is increased rapidly and credit conditions consequently made easier (lower interest rates, lower down payments on loans, etc.), the $C + I + G$ curves tend to shift upward, and vice versa.

Low interest rates and easy credit terms tend to stimulate home buying. State and local governments find such times opportune for floating bond issues and using the proceeds for investment in roads and schools. People are more freely able to borrow on automobiles and consumer durables. Easy credit terms apparently influence the investment plans of large business firms to a lesser extent, but they do have some effect. An increase in interest rates and credit terms tends to work in the opposite direction, reducing various forms of spending and especially home buying. Monetary policy, like fiscal policy, can shift the $C + I + G$ aggregate demand curves up or down, and thereby raise or lower the equilibrium level of GNP.

With this background, there are two aspects of monetary policy to be kept in mind:

*[handwritten: AD↑ GNP↑ Demand for Credit↑]*

First, when aggregate demand and GNP rise—say, because of an increase in government spending—the demand for credit also rises. Business firms need more credit to finance the increase in production. The government has increased its spending relative to its tax revenues and has to borrow money. If the government does not also act to increase the supply of money and credit, the rising demand for credit in the fact of a constant supply will cause the price of credit— i.e., interest rates—to increase. In turn the higher interest rates will tend to reduce spending and offset part of the rise in GNP that would have occurred otherwise. Unless monetary policy "accommodates" fiscal policy, therefore, *some* of the effects of that policy on GNP will be eliminated by the influence of changes in interest rates and credit terms.

Second, monetary and fiscal policy are to some extent alternative means of achieving economic stability. If GNP falls below potential, aggregate demand can be stimulated by fiscal action (lower taxes, higher expenditures) or by monetary policy (lower interest rates, easier credit). Similarly, when actual GNP runs ahead of potential GNP and inflation occurs, actual GNP may be reduced by a more restrictive fiscal policy, by a tighter monetary policy, or by a wide variety of combinations of the two.

As an example of how fiscal and monetary policy interrelate, consider the economic events of the late 1960s. Starting in late 1965, aggregate demand, stimulated by sharp increases in government spending on the Vietnam war, began to exceed potential GNP. Prices, which had been rising during the early 1960s at a gentle 1 to 1.5 per cent annual rate, began to rise at 3 to 4 per cent per year. After much debate, the Congress in July 1968 passed a tax increase, the 10 per cent surcharge. But Congress also legislated a $6 billion reduction in government spending. Fearful that the combination of the surcharge (yielding $11 billion per year in higher taxes) *and* the expenditure cut would be too stiff a dose of anti-inflationary medicine, possibly leading to a recession, the monetary authorities during the latter half of 1968 and early 1969 maintained a relatively "easy" credit policy. As a consequence, at least part of the demand-reducing effect of fiscal policy was negated by the demand-increasing effect of monetary policy on investment and consumer durable spending.

From hindsight, it now appears clear that inflationary pressures were stronger than the authorities believed and that the combined tax increase and expenditure cut was not too severe a measure of anti-inflationary fiscal policy. Because monetary policy worked in the opposite direction from fiscal policy during this period, inflation was not moderated. In the latter half of 1969 and early 1970, the combined pressure of tight money and a restrictive fiscal policy finally began to reduce the excessive aggregate demand. Actual GNP fell below potential GNP and unemployment rose.

Economists disagree to some extent on the relative efficacy of fiscal and monetary policy. Indeed, there are some who believe that monetary conditions are the dominant force in the economy and that changes in fiscal policy not accompanied by "accommodating" changes in monetary policy will have little effect on aggregate demand. The majority, however, view both tools as important, although differing over the precise magnitude of the effects to be expected from each.

## AUTOMATIC STABILIZERS
## IN THE ECONOMY

Because of the multiplier, an initial decrease in investment or other form of spending leads to a greater decline in GNP. The larger the multiplier, the greater the likelihood that an initial reduction in spending will lead to a serious economic collapse. Since World War II, fortunately, the multiplier has been relatively small during the moderate recessions the economy has experienced. There have been a number of *automatic stabilizers* at work, tending to limit the size of the multiplier. By "automatic" we mean stabilizing features in the economy that come into play without any deliberate action by the Congress or the president when recession or inflation threatens.

The size of the multiplier depends on the consumption–GNP relation, i.e. on $MPC_g$. A high $MPC_g$ means that a large proportion of any change in GNP and GNI is translated into changes in consumption spending. A low $MPC_g$ implies the opposite. There are *four* major features of our economy which tend to produce a *low* $MPC_g$ during moderate swings in GNP.

1. *Gross business saving absorbs a large part of any change in GNI*, thereby helping to stabilize disposable personal income. Profits are very sensitive to slight changes in the level of economic activity and drop off rapidly when GNP declines. Moreover, corporations attempt to maintain steady dividends, even in the face of declining profits. As a consequence, when GNP declines, retained business earnings, and hence gross business saving, fall much more rapidly than other forms of income—they absorb a large share of the decline in GNI. The converse is true when GNP is rising sharply.

2. *Government tax collections also automatically rise and fall with GNP*. Most taxes are based on the level of income, profits, or sales. As a consequence, part of the fall in GNP and GNI is absorbed by government tax revenues, leaving that much less to be absorbed by disposable personal income.

3. *When income and employment decline, government transfer payments automatically increase*. Our unemployment compensation system provides income support for those who have lost a job. As a consequence, the impact of a decline in GNP and GNI on wage income is softened by an increase in government unemployment compensation payments.

4. *Finally, to the extent that disposable personal income does decline, consumers still maintain as much of their earlier living standard as possible*. Believing that their loss of income is only temporary, many families whose income has been reduced during a recession will not cut back their consumption outlays to an extent proportionate with their income.

Because of these automatic stabilizers, the $MPC_g$ tends to be relatively small during moderate fluctuations in GNP. We have been using, for illustrative purposes earlier in this chapter, an $MPC_g$ of .6. During moderate cyclical fluctuations, the $MPC_g$ is more likely to be about .25 or .35. This yields a multiplier somewhere between 1.3 and 1.6 [The multiplier $= \dfrac{1}{- MPC_g}$.] As a consequence, initial changes in investment or government spending are less likely to lead to major depressions or inflations.

The automatic stabilizers, however, have their limits. They help to moderate declines in GNP, but they cannot in themselves achieve a recovery to full-employment conditions. Moreover, they tend to give way in the face of really major initial declines in spending. There is a limit to how long gross business

80

saving can absorb a large share of the decline in income. As a recession lengthens, dividends are cut and hence personal income falls. More and more of the unemployed exhaust their rights to unemployment insurance. And consumers themselves, faced with a long-lasting decline in their incomes, cannot maintain their earlier spending habits as their savings disappear and their credit possibilities are exhausted.

In brief, then, the automatic stabilizers significantly limit the impact on GNP of moderate fluctuations in investment or other spending. But in the face of very sharp and long-lasting reductions in outlays, the automatic stabilizers themselves tend to weaken, the multiplier becomes larger, and the ultimate fall in GNP is correspondingly greater.

## SUMMARY

That level of output will be produced which can profitably be sold. For the economy as a whole, this means that GNP will be established at that point where output is matched by aggregate demand. Although each dollar of GNP generates a dollar of GNI, this does not mean that *any* level of GNP can be exactly matched by aggregate demand. The creation of income does not guarantee the spending of income.

For every level of GNP (= GNI) there is a specific level of consumption demand. Part of GNI "leaks off" into gross business saving and taxes. The remainder goes to disposable personal income. In turn, the consumption function relates consumer spending to disposable personal income. Part of any increase in disposable income is consumed, the remainder saved. The consumption–GNP relation combines all these relations into one; it gives the level of consumption demand that will be forthcoming at each level of GNP (or GNI). The consumption–GNP relation determines $MPC_g$, which is the ratio between the *change* in consumption and the *change* in GNP. By adding investment and government demand to the consumption–GNP relation, we get a schedule of aggregate demand for each level of GNI.

At that level of GNP where the portion of GNI flowing into business saving, personal saving, and taxes is matched by the sum of investment and government purchases, the schedule of aggregate demand will equal GNP. In other words, at this point, that part of GNI *not* spent on consumer goods *is* spent on other goods. This is the equilibrium level of GNP. It is the level of GNP at which output is matched by aggregate demand.

Levels of output higher than the equilibrium level are not sustainable, since aggregate demand would be *less* than output, leaving goods unsold. Lower than equilibrium levels of GNP are not sustainable, since at these lower levels aggregate demand would exceed output.

Since any change in GNP (= GNI) is accompanied by a change in con-

81

sumption demand, an initial change in investment or government spending will lead to a larger change in GNP. The initial increase in spending leads to a rise in output and income that calls forth an increase in consumption demand, which itself leads to a further rise in income and output, and so forth. The ratio that links the ultimate change in GNP to the initial change in spending is called the multiplier. It equals $\frac{1}{1 - \text{MPC}_g}$. The higher the $\text{MPC}_g$, the larger the multiplier.

A reduction in government taxes raises the consumption–GNP relation. With taxes lower, a larger part of GNI will flow into disposable income, thereby raising the consumption–GNP relation and the aggregate demand schedule. An increase in taxes has the opposite effect. When actual GNP is below potential, government fiscal policy can raise employment and output. In such a situation, increased government spending, decreased taxes, or a combination of the two, can lead to an initial increase in purchases and, through the multiplier, to an even higher rise in GNP. Conversely, when aggregate demand exceeds potential GNP and inflation threatens, appropriate fiscal policy calls for a reduction in government spending or an increase in taxes in order to remove the excess in aggregate demand.

During periods of moderate economic fluctuations, the value of the multiplier tends to be held to a relatively small value by a series of automatic economic stabilizers. Gross business saving and government taxes absorb a large part of the change in GNI, so that fluctuations in disposable personal incomes are damped. Payment of unemployment compensation benefits softens the impact of recession on wage income. And consumers, during periods of a temporary fall in income, tend to try to maintain their former living standards. For all these reasons, the response of consumption to changes in GNI is relatively modest. But the effectiveness of the automatic stabilizers is likely to be reduced in the face of really sharp and long-lasting declines in spending. From the point of view of economic stability, this means that our economy has a good deal of resilience in withstanding the effects of modest declines in investment spending. It is more likely to react sharply to deep and persistent reductions in investment outlays.


## APPENDIX TO CHAPTER THREE

#### How GNP Is Determined:
#### An Algebraic Presentation

The determination of GNP can also be shown in simple algebraic form. Let us designate GNP and GNI as $Y$ and aggregate demand as $D$.

We can write the fact that aggregate demand is the sum of consumption, investment, and government purchases as:

$$D = C + I + G \tag{1}$$

Since in equilibrium, $Y = D$, we can write, as a condition for equilibrium:

$$Y = C + I + G \tag{2}$$

The consumption–GNP relation can be written:

$$C = a + bY \tag{3}$$
($a + bY$ is the formula for a straight line.)

The $b$ in equation (3) is the fraction of any change in GNP ($= $ GNI) that is consumed—i.e., $b = \text{MPC}_g$.

In equation (2) we can substitute the values for $C$ given by equation (3):

$$Y = a + bY + I + G \tag{4}$$

Now we have only one unknown, since $a$ and $I + G$ are given, known numbers, and we have stated $C$ in terms of $Y$. To solve, subtract $bY$ from both sides of the equation:

$$Y - bY = a + I + G \tag{5}$$

Factor out $Y$:

$$Y(1 - b) = a + I + G \tag{6}$$

Solve by dividing both sides of the equation by $(1 - b)$:

$$Y = \frac{a + I + G}{1 - b} \tag{7}$$

The equilibrium level of GNP, then, depends on the specific shape of the consumption–GNP relation (given by $a$ and $b$) and the level of investment and government spending (given by $I + G$).

A numerical example may help to illustrate the process involved. Suppose $a = 60$, $b = .6$, $I = 80$, $G = 80$. Then we have the following equation:

$$Y = C + 80 + 80 \tag{2a}$$
$$C = 60 + .6Y \tag{3a}$$

Substituting (3a) into (2a):

$$Y = 60 + .6Y + 80 + 80 \tag{4a}$$

Subtracting $.6Y$ from both sides:

$$Y - .6Y = 60 + 80 + 80 = 220 \tag{5a}$$

Factoring out $Y$:

$$Y(1 - .6) = 220 \tag{6a}$$

Solving:

$$Y = \frac{220}{1 - .6} = \frac{220}{.4} \tag{7a}$$

$$Y = 550 \tag{8a}$$

The gross national product would be $550 billion, given the consumption–GNP relation and the investment and government spending we have assumed.

More elaborate systems of equations can be devised. How would you treat gross business saving and taxes explicitly? And how would the equations change if investment were not a given constant, but a function of $Y$?

# Investment

## CHAPTER FOUR

As we saw in Chapter 3, the level of gross national product is determined by the interaction of the consumption–GNP relation with the level of investment and government spending. Throughout the history of modern industrial countries major changes in GNP have been associated with changes in investment spending. Investment has fluctuated sharply, and through the multiplier, these fluctuations have resulted in even larger absolute changes in total spending and output. To understand this force, which has often caused GNP to fall below its potential with the attendant unemployment of men and machines and to surge up against potential in an inflationary boom, we must examine the factors influencing investment decisions. That is the primary task of this chapter.

Aside from the massive swings in government expenditures that occur in wartime, investment is the most volatile component of GNP. The production and installation of equipment and the construction of buildings and public works add to the nation's stock of productive capital. But these additions do not often come in a steady stream. More usually they increase rapidly for a number of years and then decline sharply. Each of the major depressions in American economic history—the 1870s, the 1890s, 1907, 1921, and, above all, the 1930s—is associated with a severe decline in investment activity. There were other dips in investment between the major declines, but these were not so severe, and correspondingly were accompanied by much more moderate downturns in over-all economic activity. Figure 4–1 presents a view of private investment spending in the United States since 1909.

We shall consider in turn each of the major kinds of investment:

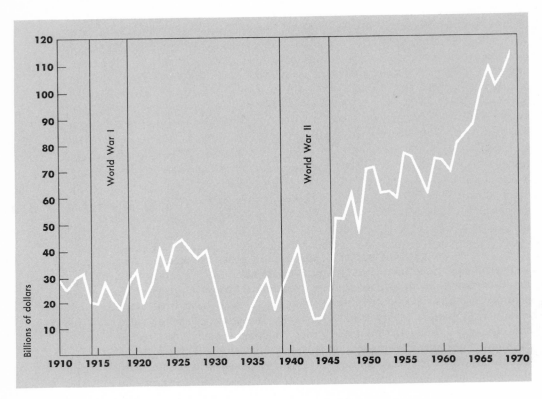

FIG. 4-1 Gross private domestic investment in the United States, 1910–1969 (in constant dollars)

*business purchases of plant and equipment, changes in business inventories, and residential construction.*

*types of investment*

## BUSINESS PURCHASES OF PLANT AND EQUIPMENT

Innovations and Investment

Business investment is perhaps the major carrier of economic change. New ideas and new methods of production are typically incorporated in new machines and improved plants. In the nineteenth century the railroads changed the face of America, not only by the transportation they provided and the new markets they created, but also by the investment they required. Railroads meant rails to be laid, rivers and streams to be bridged, pig iron and steel to be poured, engines and cars to be constructed, and freight yards to be built. The introduction and expansion of electric utilities required and, indeed, still require, vast purchases of generating equipment, power lines, and transformer stations. The major innovations in economic activity—railroads, electric utilities, petroleum, the automobile, and others—have carried with them waves of new investment activity, at first swelling and then receding. Not all, or even the majority, of business investment at any given time is directly associated with the development of new industries or products. But the investment that is stimulated by major innovations has indirect influences throughout the economy. In periods when *innovational investment* is substantial and rising, economic expansion is less likely to be interrupted by serious depression than in other periods. Not only is investment strong in the innovating industry itself, but the investment plans of firms that supply the innovating industry with materials and equipment are also likely to be ambitious. On the other hand, when a wave of innovational investment is completed, the subsequent decline in total investment may be doubly serious. As investment by a major innovational industry begins to slacken, its purchases of plant and equipment falter; the expansion of activity in the machinery and construction industries is slowed, if not reversed. This is soon reflected in a slowing down of sales expansion in such older supplying industries as steel and building materials. As a consequence, the investment of these industries is likely to decline, adding even greater downward pressure to the fall in total investment and GNP.

#### Expectations and Investment

Investment directly involves expectations about the future. The purchase of plant and equipment is not an end in itself. These assets are valuable to the investing firm because they are a means of production, and hence an instrument for future sales and profits. The key word in the last sentence is future. Business fixed assets are long-lived. The revenue derived from them stretches, in the usual case, over many years. An act of investment, therefore, is based on the calculation that the contribution of the asset to sales and profits will more than repay its cost by a sufficient margin to make its acquisition worthwhile. Whether a given investment is made or not, therefore, depends on expectations about its profitability in the years ahead.

Businessmen's expectations about the future thus play a major role in determining the volume of investment. Current events, of course, shape our hopes and fears about future events; expectations about tomorrow are grounded not on pure imagination, but at least in part on what is happening today, and on the experience of the recent past. Business expectations do not usually undergo wild and unpredictable swings. Nevertheless, there are times when expectations do change radically. Thus a deterioration in economic conditions that might otherwise be moderate and temporary might lead to more serious trouble if businessmen began to project the current decline as deepening in the future. Such a collapse in ex-

87

pectations is particularly likely if it has been preceded by a speculative boom in which expectations rose to unwarranted heights.

Our discussion so far has identified two features of investment behavior that make it subject to fluctuations—its association with innovation and its dependence on expectations about the future. But these are only general characteristics; they do not tell us *specifically* how investment is likely to behave in any given set of economic circumstances. Yet this is what we must know in order to understand the anatomy of cyclical fluctuations in GNP. For that purpose we turn to a systematic examination of the investment decisions of business firms and of the effects of economic events on them. There are two key factors we shall have to consider as major determinants of investment: business *sales* (actual and expected) and business *profits*.

### Fixed Capital Per Unit of Output

Along with labor and raw materials, almost all production requires a stock of *fixed capital* in the form of buildings and equipment. Investment occurs when firms purchase capital goods either for replacement or for making net additions to their stock of capital. But what determines the size of the capital stock with which business firms desire to operate? As an initial approximation we can say that a firm's total stock of capital will depend, first, on how much capital it decides to use per unit of output, and second, on the volume of output it decides to produce. Thus if the most efficient production technique calls for $2 million of plant and equipment for each $1 million of annual output, and a firm has annual sales and output of $20 million, then the stock of fixed capital it requires is $40 million. Its *capital–output ratio* is 2. Table 4–1 shows the capital–output ratios of major industries in the U.S. in 1962. During the postwar period, capital–output ratios have declined gradually, as capital has become more efficient. Equipment has become more productive and great economies have been realized in the design and use of factory buildings.

At first, the amount of capital that is appropriate for a given output would seem to be mainly an engineering question. To produce a million tons of steel, for example, a certain number of blast furnaces and rolling mills are necessary. Heat-treating facilities and rolling-mill equipment must be available, and so forth. As a matter of fact, however, the amount of capital appropriate for a specific output is as much an economic as a technical problem. There are usually several different techniques available for producing any particular commodity. Which one is preferable will generally depend on which one yields the greatest profit return on the capital invested. Imagine two production techniques: the one, call it *A*, requires little labor but heavy investment in complicated machinery; the other, *B*, uses more labor but simpler and less costly equipment. Choosing *A* rather than *B* means, in effect, using more capital and less labor. The lower the price of machinery and the cheaper the cost of obtaining investment funds, the

88

**Table 4–1   CAPITAL–OUTPUT RATIOS, U.S. INDUSTRIES, 1962**

| Industry or Sector | 1962 |
|---|---|
| Total manufacturing | .66 |
| Primary metals | 1.38 |
| Machinery | .34 |
| Motor vehicles | .48 |
| Nonautomotive transportation equipment | .42 |
| Stone, clay, and glass | .79 |
| Other durables | .39 |
| Food and beverages | .42 |
| Textiles | .81 |
| Paper | .83 |
| Chemicals | .68 |
| Petroleum and coal | 2.28 |
| Rubber | .52 |
| Other nondurables | .22 |
| Railroads | 4.63 |
| Nonrail transportation | .70 |
| Public utilities | 3.54 |
| Communications | 1.73 |
| Commercial and other | .65 |
| Farming | 2.57 |
| All industries covered by the study | 1.01 |

Source: Bert G. Hickman, *Investment Demand & U.S. Economic Growth* (Washington, D.C.: The Brookings Institution, 1965), p. 152.

more likely it is that technique *A* will be chosen over *B*. And the higher the wage rate, the greater will be the saving in labor costs provided by the manpower economies under technique *A*. Whether *A* or *B* will be chosen, therefore, will depend on the price of capital goods and the wages of labor, as well as the technical engineering possibilities.

New production techniques usually have to be embodied in new and more advanced equipment. In general, the progress of science and technology in its application to industry has developed increasingly efficient forms of fixed capital. This in turn has favored the use of more capital relative to labor in production. However, the speed with which improvements are adopted depends on the price of the capital equipment and the cost of financing it, compared to the wages of the labor for which it can be substituted. Over the years, the price of labor has risen steadily relative to the price of capital goods. This fact, in combination with the improved efficiency of capital, has led to a continued increase in the amount of capital relative to labor.

In summary, then, the amount of capital per unit of output which it will be efficient for a firm to use depends on: (1) the progress and the character of new technology; (2) the price of capital goods and the cost of obtaining funds to purchase them; and (3) the wages of labor for which the capital can potentially be substituted.

89

Given the optimum amount of capital per unit of production, the total stock of capital that a firm finds desirable will depend on the size of its markets—in other words, on its production and sales. If we know how much capital is required per unit of output, then total capital requirements are simply that amount times the number of units produced. Thus the desired stock of capital depends on the expected volume of production. *If production were to be stable for an extended period, no further additions to fixed capital would be desired.* As existing capital wears out, some purchases of plant and equipment will occur for replacement purposes, but no net investment will take place. (Remember that net investment represents *additions* to the stock of capital.)

Rising sales and output will raise the desired stock of capital, however, and the firm will purchase new machinery, over and above its replacement requirements. The faster the rate of increase in sales and output, the larger the net investment required to keep the capital stock up to the desired level. Should the rate of increase in sales slow down, even though it remains positive, the level of investment will decline. This is one of the major sources of investment instability. *The level of investment is very sensitive to the rate of increase in GNP* and has a tendency to decline, even at high levels of economic activity, if the rate of growth of GNP should falter. *This relation between the level of investment and the rate of growth in GNP is called the "accelerator,"* because variations in investment depend on the acceleration or deceleration of GNP. This phenomenon calls attention to the fact that it is a high rate of growth, rather than a high level, of sales and economic activity which promotes a large volume of business investment.

Table 4–2 illustrates the acceleration principle applied to an individual firm. Suppose a firm finds it most efficient to produce with techniques that require $2 million of plant and equipment for each $1 million of output. Then, a production and sales volume of $20 million would require a capital stock of $40 million. Let us also assume that each year $3 million in new machinery or plant must be purchased simply to maintain the existing capital. So long as sales stay at $20

Table 4–2   THE ACCELERATOR PRINCIPLE APPLIED
TO AN INDIVIDUAL FIRM (Millions of Dollars)

| Year | Sales | Desired Level of Capital | Net Investment | Replacement Investment | Total Investment |
|------|-------|--------------------------|----------------|------------------------|------------------|
| 1 | $20 | $40 | $0 | $3 | $3 |
| 2 | 20 | 40 | 0 | 3 | 3 |
| 3 | 21 | 42 | 2 | 3 | 5 |
| 4 | 24 | 48 | 6 | 3 | 9 |
| 5 | 27 | 54 | 6 | 3 | 9 |
| 6 | 29 | 58 | 4 | 3 | 7 |
| 7 | 30 | 60 | 2 | 3 | 5 |
| 8 | 30 | 60 | 0 | 3 | 3 |
| 9 | 28½ | 57 | —3 | 3 | 0 |

million per year, no net additions to capital are required, and total investment consists merely of replacement purchases. However, as sales begin to expand, new capital is required. A $1 million expansion in sales leads to net investment of $2 million; a $3 million sales expansion calls forth net investment of $6 million.

*Total* investment by the firm is the sum of net investment and replacement ~~total investment~~ investment. Notice in Table 4–2 that total investment reaches its peak (in years 4 and 5) when sales are expanding most rapidly. Thereafter, as the increase in sales becomes smaller, investment declines. When sales level off, even though they are much higher than formerly, net investment drops to zero. Finally, in year 9, when sales decline, the desired capital stock is reduced, and net investment is negative—the firm lets its capital stock run down by not making the normal $3 million replacement requirement.[1]

The table also illustrates one of the reasons why the output of investment goods fluctuates more than the output of other goods. In the business firm of our example (say, a firm producing consumer goods), sales rose from $20 million to $30 million and fell back to $28.5 million, a rise of 50 per cent followed by a decline of 5 per cent. But the sales of the firms producing machinery and equipment first rose by 300 per cent and then fell to zero!

The fact that the level of investment tends to be influenced by the rate of growth in sales—i.e., the accelerator principle—should not be taken to mean that the rate of growth in sales is the only factor determining investment. Even if sales were not growing at all, so that there was no need to invest for purposes of expanding capacity, business firms might still undertake investment in order to *modernize* capacity. The discovery of new technology can stimulate modernization investment by making available new types of machinery and equipment that promise to cut costs and raise profits. A rise in wage rates relative to the price of new machinery can make profitable some investments in labor-saving machinery which, at the old wage rates, were not quite profitable enough to warrant undertaking. In short, business firms invest both to expand their capital stock and to modernize it.[2] Neither motive is the sole explanation for investment.

### Profits and Investment

Business firms invest to make a profit. In the case of accelerator investment, undertaken to meet an increase in sales, capacity is added not for its own sake but because the firm expects to increase its profits from the higher sales which the capacity expansion will make possible. When a firm introduces new cost-reducing equipment, it does so because it expects that the saving in labor or material costs

[1] Notice that negative net investment ("disinvestment") occurs through failure to replace. Hence it can never be larger. than replacement requirements; this limits the rate at which disinvestment can occur.

[2] Any given act of investment—say, the construction of a new factory—may represent both elements of investment. The factory may be required as a capacity addition to meet growing sales volume and may also be substantially more modern, more capital-using, and more labor-saving than older factories owned by the same firm.

will exceed the cost of the new equipment and that its profits will thereby be increased. Although *expected profits* are the major incentive for investment, *current profits* are an important source of funds out of which the firm finances its investment. Profits, therefore, play a dual role in the investment process as both an incentive and a source of funds.

Strictly speaking, it is the expectation of future profits that is important from the viewpoint of *incentives* to invest. In considering whether a particular investment is sufficiently profitable to warrant undertaking, it is the profit that it will earn in the future that is relevant. A firm may be making very poor profits on its existing capital, and yet because of access to a new production technique, for example, it may have an excellent opportunity to make a profitable new investment. Conversely, at the top of an economic boom a firm may be currently earning very high profits, yet its management, forecasting an end to the boom and a decline in sales, may be reluctant to expand capacity. The current level of profits, therefore, is not an *infallible* guide to the profits that could be earned on new investment. But it is, nevertheless, an important indicator of future profitability. If profits on the current volume of sales are high, barring specific evidence to the contrary, it is quite likely that firms will expect investment in capacity expansion to yield high profits in the future. Moreover, when current profits are high, business management tends to be optimistic. In evaluating the profitability of new investment, management is more likely to discount the risks and emphasize the opportunities. As a consequence, even though there is no neat mechanical relation between current profits on existing capital and those obtained from new investment, a high level of current profits is likely to encourage investment.

Although expected profits are an incentive for new investment, current profits furnish a major *source of funds* to finance it. In most corporations only part of the profits remaining after payment of taxes are distributed to stockholders as dividends. (At the present time about 50 per cent of corporate profits after taxes is paid out in dividends.) The remainder is available to be plowed back into the firm in the form of investment in plant, equipment, research, and development. And, in addition to retained profits, the firm has another *internal* source of investment funds; namely, the depreciation it deducted in computing its net profits. These two forms of internal funds—retained profits and depreciation—are available to finance new investment. Business firms, of course, do raise funds in other ways. They can borrow, through a bank loan or a bond flotation, or they can issue new stock. However, most firms are reluctant to increase their debt or their outstanding issues of stock too rapidly. In general, internal sources of funds are a preferred source of capital for financing investment. There is no ironclad rule about this. And even when there are ample sources of funds available, firms will not invest if they do not foresee a profitable outcome to the venture. Nevertheless, this general preference for internal sources of funds does mean that an expanding level of profits is likely to be associated with an increase in investment, and vice versa.

The association between changes in profits and changes in investment, explored in the last few paragraphs, is yet another reason for the wide swings in investment that have characterized the economic history of industrialized countries. Of all the forms of income, profits tend to fluctuate most sharply. They rise more in booms and fall more in recessions. As a result, this key source of investible funds—and of business psychology—varies strongly with the business cycle, helping to make investment the most volatile component of GNP.

Economists tend to disagree among themselves about the relative importance of changes in sales (the accelerator) on the one hand, and the level of profits on the other, in explaining fluctuations in investment. Some believe that the preference of business management for financing investment through internal sources of funds is weak, but that changes in sales automatically carry with them the promise of satisfactory profits on expanded capacity. As a consequence, they believe that the accelerator is the major explanation for investment fluctuations. Conversely, of course, those who stress the importance of management's preference for internal sources of finance tend to emphasize the role of profits as a determinant of investment. It is difficult to settle the dispute from the available statistics. As in most such cases, there appears to be some truth in both contentions. To explain the fluctuations in investment we must take into account both the change in sales relative to existing capacity and the level of profits.

Although business firms rely principally on internally generated profits as a means to finance investment, they meet some of their investment financing requirements from borrowed funds. As a consequence, the level of interest rates and other terms and conditions of borrowing affect the volume of business investment. The higher the level of interest rates, the smaller are the profits from an investment that the firm can keep, and the less attractive, therefore, are investments that must be financed with borrowed funds. Precisely how strongly changes in interest rates affect the over-all level of business investment is another matter about which economists are not in agreement. In the late 1930s and during the first decade after World War II, there was a tendency among most economists to minimize the effect of interest rate changes on business investment (while still realizing that interest rates and credit conditions did have an influence on home building and purchases of consumer durables). More recently, there has been more of an inclination among economists to give interest rates a somewhat larger, though by no means a dominant role, in explaining the level of business investment.[3]

[3] A number of recent statistical studies of the determinants of business investment have concluded that interest rates do have a role to play. Isolating the influence of interest rates on investment requires relatively sophisticated statistical tools. Historically, interest rates have been high precisely at a time when profits were high and sales advancing rapidly. Both these latter factors tend to *increase* investment. Hence, simply looking at the raw statistical data, one might conclude that high interest rates were associated with high levels of investment, rather than vice versa. It took the development of relatively sophisticated statistical techniques to begin disentangling the various influences on investment, and even now there is much that we do not know.

If we start with the proposition that the ultimate reason firms undertake investment is to add to their profits, we can summarize the major factors influencing investment as shown schematically in Table 4–3.

### Table 4–3  MAJOR FACTORS INFLUENCING INVESTMENT

| Economic Event | How the Event Affects Profit Expectations | Impact on Investment Decisions |
|---|---|---|
| Sales growth | Profits can be increased by building new capacity | Accelerator investment undertaken to expand capacity |
| Technological advance; wage rate increases | Profits can be increased by modernization and labor-saving investment | Modernization and labor-saving investment undertaken |
| High level of current profits | Calculation of future profits and sales more likely to be optimistic | Doubts about profitability of accelerator and modernization investment resolved in favor of undertaking investment |
| | Internal funds available for investment are plentiful; consequently, real and psychological costs of financing investment are reduced; net profit expectations increased | Financial cost and other financial obstacles to accelerator and modernization investment reduced |
| Low interest rates | Net profit expectations (after interest payments) of investment projects increased | Accelerator and modernization investment stimulated |

## DAMPENERS
## ON THE ACCELERATOR

So far, our discussion of investment has emphasized its instability. According to accelerator theory, declines in investment begin when the rate of growth in sales slows down. For the economy as a whole this implies that whenever a boom starts to lose its steam, a downturn in economic activity would soon follow. The decline in investment, resulting from a slower rate of growth, would itself lead to a still further slowdown in GNP as the multiplier took hold. As purchases of investment goods were reduced, wages, profits, and other incomes in the capital goods industries would fall. Through the consumption function, this would lead to reduction in consumer purchases, to cuts in production and income in consumer-goods industries, still lower incomes, and so on. Falling profits would further discourage new investment, as would the sharp decline in business expectations about the future that would surely accompany such a decline in GNP. An initial slowdown in the rate of economic growth would inevitably lead to a subsequent sharp decline in output, income, and employment.

If investment behaved as the accelerator theory indicates, we would indeed have an extremely unstable economy. Major depressions and wild booms would follow swiftly one upon the other. Increases in economic activity would feed upon themselves, as increases in sales led to increases in investment and, through the multiplier, to even larger increases in sales. The slowing down of this process as the economy reached the limits of its productive capacity would throw the whole machine into reverse, bringing on depression. A strong underlying trend of innovational investment might sustain the economy and prevent a mild recession from turning into a deep depression. But this would be fortuitous. And, given the accelerator mechanism, even a mild slackening in the strength of innovational investment could lead, through a reduction in the rate of growth in GNP, to a major economic collapse.

In actual fact, however, our economy is not that unstable. We have suffered, indeed, major depressions. But there were fairly long periods between such depressions. More important, most mild recessions did not turn into major depressions. During these recessions, business sales declined moderately. Investment purchases also fell, but did not decline as precipitously as the accelerator theory would have predicted. Clearly there must be factors other than those we have described so far which keep investment from being so extremely sensitive to current changes in business sales and profits.

### Sales Expectations

An increase in sales that is expected to be *temporary* will not normally induce business firms to expand their capacity. Purchasing additional plant and equipment to meet a temporary rise in sales would merely leave the firm with expensive excess capacity in the years ahead. A temporary sales increase can be better met by working overtime or adding to the work force and using existing capacity more intensively. In this way the firm will not be saddled with permanently higher costs when sales decline again, since the overtime can then be eliminated or the extra employees laid off.

In other words, only an increase in sales expected to be *permanent* will induce firms to undertake costly additions to their fixed assets. This substantially weakens the force of the accelerator. As sales rise sharply during a boom, only part of the increase will normally be considered as permanent, and hence the investment response will be moderate. After all, most firms have had long experience with the ups and downs of the business cycle. Since capacity is not raised as fast as the temporary sales rise during the boom, there may still be a need for additional capacity, and consequently for investment, when sales level off. And should sales decline, the amount of excess capacity will not be quite so great.

In 1968 and 1969, the increase in business investment was significantly larger than earlier predictions. One reason for the surprising strength of investment may have been that the relation between actual sales and businessmen's expectations of future sales had changed in the 1960s. By early 1969, the American economy had experienced eight years of uninterrupted prosperity and sales expansion. Never before in our history had the economy advanced for so many years without even a minor recession. In earlier periods of rapid economic advance, business firms discounted some of the increase in sales as a temporary phenomenon, expecting at least part of the increase to be wiped out by a recession in the near future. But after eight consecutive years of steady sales growth, they may have become less cautious and, as a consequence, more ready to undertake capacity expansion and modernization. Although there is no means of testing this hypothesis at the moment—since the presumed change in attitudes is so recent—it may offer a reasonable explanation for the behavior of investment in 1968 and 1969.

### Lags and Backlogs

Investment takes time to accomplish. Even after a business firm decides to undertake a major investment project, the actual process of ordering, producing, and installing new machinery and equipment usually stretches over a long period of time. A generator for an electric power plant may take 18 to 24 months to produce and install; building a new blast furnace is not accomplished overnight. Thus, when sales increase and business firms decide on an expansion of capacity, or when a decision is made to adopt a new production technique, the investment consequences will usually stretch out over a considerable period of time. Conversely, when sales increases begin to slacken and dip, investment will fall off more gradually, as projects initiated earlier are still being brought to completion. This results in a smoother path for total investment outlays and hence for the resulting income payments. The impact on the economy is thereby dampened.

A similar "stretching out" of the investment process occurs, especially during prosperous periods, simply because of the limited ability of any organization to adapt to change. Capacity expansions or improvements in production techniques place added burdens on management, require the retraining of old personnel or the hiring of new, often mean expanding the sales and marketing departments of the firm, and so on. Frequently, in the early stages of operation, new capacity is not yet "broken in"; costly delays and other inefficiencies result. As a consequence, there is a limit to how fast the typical firm will find it profitable to invest. This limit further reduces the pace of investment below what might otherwise be expected during periods of rapid increases in sales.

### Interest Rates and the Availability of Credit

As a general rule, when sales increase rapidly, business profits and retained earnings also expand. This expansion makes it easier for firms to finance additional investment. But for investment to increase during such periods as sharply as the accelerator theory predicts (see the example in Table 4–2), most firms would have to increase sharply their reliance on outside sources of funds. And this very fact tends to limit the rise in investment.

In the first place, business firms are always reluctant to take on sizable increases in debt. Moreover, during periods of general economic prosperity credit becomes tighter. Interest rates rise and lenders screen prospective borrowers more closely. It is more difficult and more costly for firms to borrow in periods of general economic expansion. Investments will only be undertaken if the expected rate of return exceeds the cost of capital, the interest rate. As the interest rate rises during prosperous periods, some marginal projects are not undertaken because their expected rate of return falls short of the high interest rates.[4] They are postponed to periods in which credit is less costly to obtain. The converse is true during periods of recession, when credit normally becomes more easily available and interest rates decline.[5]

### Backlog of Investment Projects

We have, so far, given at least four reasons why investment actually undertaken during prosperous periods will tend to lag behind the investment opportunities being created during these periods:

1. When sales rise, firms are wary at first and, before expanding their plant and equipment fully in line with the increased sales, wait to see if the gain in sales is "permanent."

2. It takes time to make decisions, order the plant or equipment, and get it produced. Hence at any time there is a "pipeline" of uncompleted investment; the bigger the boom the greater the volume of investment projects in the pipeline.

3. Management can only absorb efficiently so much new plant and equipment at a time. Hence even though new investment opportunities may be opening up rapidly, actual purchases of investment goods occur more gradually.

4. Investment may be "stretched out" over time due to a shortage of internal funds and the high cost of borrowed funds. Management will go to the outside market for funds, but their reluctance to do so, combined with the higher costs of borrowing during periods of general prosperity, may result in the postponement of some marginal projects until a later time.

For all these reasons, the volume of investment actually undertaken tends to be less than the investment opportunities opened up when sales and profits are

[4]See J. S. Duesenberry, *Money and Credit*, 2nd ed., another book in this Series, for a full discussion of the effect of the interest rate on investment.

[5]In the early stages of the depression of the 1930s, the collapse of the banking system and the failure of many other financial institutions resulted in a severe tightening of credit. The collapse of investment was intensified by the sharp contraction of credit availability. The depression of 1907 was set off by a financial "panic," and here again credit tightened rather than eased. More usually, however, a recession or depression is accompanied by easier money and lower interest rates.

rising sharply. As a consequence, during a period of rising economic activity there is often created a *backlog of unexploited investment possibilities.* When sales and profits begin to level off and decline, the existence of a backlog of investment projects tends to moderate the fall in investment outlays that would otherwise occur. *This does not mean that investment is stable.* It does typically fluctuate more than consumption or government spending. But it will not move up and down as violently as the accelerator theory suggests. In particular, every minor recession need not turn into a major one. The mere fact that sales cease to rise, and then decline for a while, does not send investment plummeting toward zero, as is implied by the simple accelerator theory. Although business investment in plant and equipment during the postwar period has fluctuated proportionately more than total GNP, it still remained at a respectable figure during the four postwar recessions.

The existence of a backlog of unexploited investment opportunities does give the economy some resistance against the occurrence of major depressions. But, of course, it does not make the economic system depression-proof. The fact that major depressions have occurred is evidence enough of this. If investment opportunities decline far enough and stay down long enough, the projects in the backlog will become less and less attractive. Moreover, with no new investment opportunities entering one side of the pipeline, and investment projects continuing to come out of the other, the pipeline is soon emptied. Then the vicious spiral of lower sales leading to lower investment, and lower investment (through the multiplier) leading to still lower sales, can take hold.


## CHANGES IN BUSINESS INVENTORIES
## (INVENTORY INVESTMENT)

A modern industrial economy not only requires plant, equipment, and manpower in order to turn out goods and services, it must also have a considerable quantity of commodities in the various pipelines of production, flowing from mines to factories to wholesalers to stores. Most producers must carry an inventory of materials, goods-in-process, and finished goods. When firms add to their inventories, production exceeds sales; when inventories are declining, production is less than sales. Thus, the rate at which business firms are increasing or decreasing their inventories has a direct effect on production and GNP. Inventory investment can change very quickly from a substantial positive amount to a large negative amount. The task of this section is to examine the reasons for this instability.

### Why Businessmen Hold Inventories

98     Holding inventories is both a necessity and a convenience for business firms. Manufacturers must have sufficient inventories of *raw materials* on hand in order

to avoid the interruptions to production that would occur if a completely "hand-to-mouth" buying policy were followed. *Goods-in-process* inventories are also necessary. The delivery of a military aircraft to the government, for example, is preceded by a long period in which the aircraft is being constructed. At each stage in the process the unfinished aircraft represents goods-in-process inventory. Finally, many manufacturers carry stocks of *finished goods* in order to avoid delays in filling customer orders. And, of course, the major function of most retailers and wholesalers is to have an extensive stock of all kinds of goods on hand in order to provide purchasers with an array of goods from which to choose. Carrying too small an inventory can be costly in terms of production delays or unsatisfied customers.

But carrying large inventories is also costly. It ties up funds on which interest must be paid and it requires storage space; perishable goods can spoil while in stock. Hence business firms must normally strike a balance between carrying sufficient inventories to meet their needs, and avoiding the costs of excessive inventories.[6] Planning the appropriate inventory policy, particularly when a wide range of different commodities is involved, is a complicated problem. The intricacies of inventory management, however, are not our concern. What we are interested in are the major factors that cause inventories to be increased or decreased and thus give rise to fluctuations in inventory investment.

As a first approximation, we can say that when sales are expected to rise, business firms will want to carry higher inventories. If production is to be increased, larger stocks of raw materials will have to be available to prevent production shutdowns. Higher production will mean more goods tied up at various stages of completion in the production process itself. And business firms will also want to hold larger stocks of finished goods in order to be able to continue to meet, without delay, the higher volume of customer orders. Lower sales and orders will, of course, tend to induce business firms to hold smaller inventories.

### Why Inventory Investment Is Unstable

It is the *change* in inventories, not the level of inventories, of course, that enters the GNP accounts, since only the change in inventories requires production. So long as the level of inventories is constant, no matter how high that level is, extra production is not required; production equals sales, and inventory investment is zero.

If inventories tend to rise and fall with sales, then *inventory investment (the change in inventories) will tend to be positive when sales are increasing and negative when sales are decreasing*. Furthermore, the more rapidly sales are increasing and the more firmly businessmen are convinced that the increases will continue into the future, the more swiftly they will try to add to their inventories

[6]The major exception to this occurs during periods when prices are expected to rise sharply. In such situations firms may often "speculate" in inventories by carrying more than they need in the hope of profiting by the price rise.

so as not to be caught short at the higher sales level. But, on reflection, this simply means that inventory investment will follow the acceleration principle outlined earlier! Rapid increases in orders and sales mean *large additions* to inventory; constant sales mean *zero additions* to inventories; declining sales mean *reductions* in inventories. Consequently, inventory investment will be heaviest when economic activity is rising most rapidly; inventory investment will decrease, but will still be positive, when the sales rise becomes smaller. And inventory investment will be negative when sales decrease.

Unlike plant and equipment, inventories can be changed fairly rapidly. Mistakes in inventory policy can be corrected much more quickly than mistakes in plant and equipment purchases. Suppose, for example, a firm has an inventory turnover four times a year; in other words, sales are sufficient, in three months, to equal inventories. Suppose, also, that sales are expected to rise by 33 per cent, and that the firm therefore increases its inventories by one-third. If it turns out that the expectations of a sales increase are wrong, and that sales do not rise, the firm can reduce its inventories back to the old level simply by ceasing its purchases of goods for a month. A similar mistake in plant and equipment purchases, however, would lead to excess capacity that could continue for a number of years. The whole point of this is that inventories can be adjusted quickly to sales changes, without the long delays and lags that accompany fixed investment in plant and equipment. As a consequence, inventory investment more closely follows an accelerator pattern than does fixed investment; it can swing from large positive amounts to large negative amounts very rapidly.

This is the basic reason why inventory investment is the most unstable component of GNP. Indeed, in moderate recessions a very large part of the decline in output represents a drop in inventory investment, rather than a change in sales to final users. This is brought out in Fig. 4–2, which compares the change in inventory investment to the change in sales to final users during the four recessions that have occurred in the postwar period. Negative inventory investment led to more cutbacks in production than the total of final sales for consumption, fixed investment, and government. Indeed, in two of the recessions, final sales did not decline at all; inventory investment accounted for all of the decline in production. In major depressions, however, inventory investment still plays a role, but it is a relatively minor one compared to the very substantial changes in other components of GNP, especially of fixed investment.

There is another feature of inventory investment that makes it very sensitive to economic fluctuations and contributes to its instability. When one firm increases its inventories, it must place orders with its suppliers. Conversely, a decrease in inventories leads to a reduction in orders flowing to suppliers. Suppose retail sales decline by 5 per cent. Retailers must reduce their orders from finished-goods manufacturers by 5 per cent simply in order to match the decline in sales. If they wish, in addition, to reduce their inventories, they must cut their orders to their manufacturing suppliers by more than 5 per cent. As a conse-

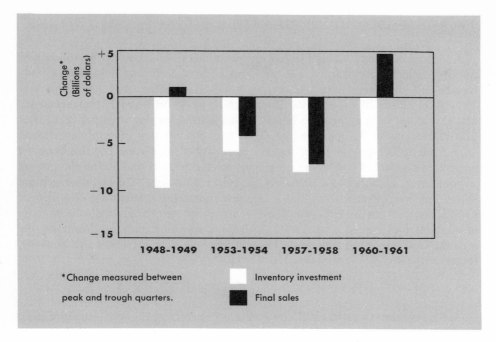

FIG. 4–2 Changes in inventory investment compared to changes in final sales during postwar recessions

quence, the sales of such manufacturers are reduced by more than 5 per cent—say, by 10 per cent. As they in turn reduce inventories, by an amount based on their own 10 per cent sales decrease, their orders to parts suppliers or raw-material producers are cut back by more than 10 per cent. And so the process is magnified as the initial sales decline cascades through the production line. Thus as we go back down the various stages of production, the sales decline is increased and, consequently, so is the inventory reduction. The final reduction in inventories, therefore, is much larger than one based solely on the 5 per cent cut in retail sales. The reverse holds true, of course, for sales increases.

When prices are expected to change, business inventory investment will also be affected. The expectation of a price increase will make it profitable for firms to buy now in order to sell at a higher price later. Indeed, if enough firms believe that prices are going to rise, prices will rise. As they all rush to purchase goods to increase their inventories, the surge of new buying will drive prices up. The opposite holds true of an expected price drop. Under normal peacetime conditions in the United States these speculative "binges" have not played an important role. A major exception was in late 1950 and early 1951 at the beginning of the Korean War, when expectations of higher prices gave rise to an inventory policy, which in turn helped create still higher prices.

# RESIDENTIAL CONSTRUCTION

Each year during the past 20 years, between 1.1 and 1.6 million new dwelling units were constructed in the United States, including both single-family houses and apartment units. At current prices, 1.5 million new units represent some $26 billion of production. Construction work on repairs, improvements, and alterations adds another $5 billion to this figure, bringing the total up to over $30 billion, about 3.5 per cent of GNP and one quarter of total investment.

Shelter, like food and clothing, is a necessity of life for all. But this does not mean that residential construction depends solely, or even mainly, on the growth in population. Houses and apartments can be small or large. They can incorporate all the modern conveniences or be a decaying slum. New families can live in their own home, or "double up" with relatives. In other words, although an increase in population ultimately does lead to a demand for additional housing units, the quantity and quality of new units built in any one year can vary substantially, whatever the increase in new families may be.

### Cyclical Fluctuations in Housing Demand

The volume of residential construction has fluctuated very sharply during the past hundred years. In 1925, for example, there were almost a million new housing units started; by 1933 the number had fallen to 93,000, only 9 per cent of the 1925 level. Even in the postwar period, which has been relatively stable in terms of over-all economic activity, new housing starts have changed by as much as 25 per cent from one year to the next.

The demand for new housing responds to changes in the number of new families, to changes in income levels, and to the volume of internal migration. Clearly, the larger the number of new families, the higher the demand for new housing. As income rises, more families can afford to have their own homes instead of living with relatives, and others will upgrade their present housing by moving into larger and more elaborately furnished homes. And the more people move from one area to another, the greater the national demand for housing, because the stimulating effect in the areas into which they are moving will not be fully offset by less building in the declining areas; some houses will simply be abandoned and hence be lost to the effective stock of dwellings that house our population.

### "Long Cycles" in Housing Construction

The behavior of residential construction in the period between the Civil War and World War II led many economists to conclude that there is a "long cycle" in residential construction of about 20 years' duration from peak to peak. In Fig. 4–3 expenditures on residential construction are shown from 1871 to 1965. (A five-year moving average has been used to smooth out the smaller year-to-year fluctuations.) Notice the peaks in 1888, 1907, and 1926, about 20 years apart. But notice also that this tendency for long periods of increase, followed by sharp decreases, has not been followed in the postwar period.

Residential construction is subject to long-term and very sizable fluctuations for several reasons. The nature of the market for housing is such that new construction often overexpands relative to the basic demand and remains high even after demand has fallen. The number of new houses built in any single year is only a small part of the total stock of housing in existence. A million new units adds less than 2 per cent to the total supply. Consequently, a small excess amount of building in one year makes little difference to the total stock; a 200,000 excess in one year, for example, represents only 0.4 per cent of the stock. And since each house, or group of houses, is to some extent unique, and each different area has its own special market, an excess of building may continue for quite some time before landlords and builders recognize the fact and react by reducing construction. After such an overshoot, the size of the required decrease in construction is, of course, all the larger.

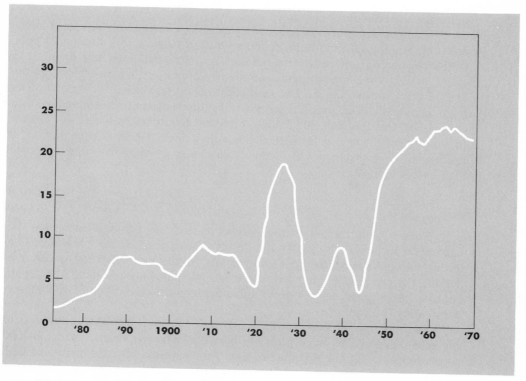

FIG. 4–3   Residential construction since 1871 (five-year moving average centered on final year; expenditures in constant dollars)

The same kind of situation exists in reverse for an upturn in construction. After a long period of low construction, a shortage of housing sets in. But, for the reasons noted above, it may be some time before the shortage leads to an increased volume of home building. A backlog of needs is built up that sustains construction for a number of years.

## Housing and Credit

The volume of residential construction depends more heavily on the availability of credit and the level of interest rates than do other forms of investment. Most houses are heavily financed by credit. As a consequence, a relatively modest change in the interest rate that borrowers have to pay raises monthly payments significantly. And when credit becomes tight, lenders often ration credit by cutting the period to maturity of the mortgages they are willing to make and by raising the down payment. In such cases, monthly payments are further increased, discouraging a number of potential home buyers. Most residential builders also depend heavily on the availability of credit to finance their costs during the period of construction. Hence in a period of tight credit, some builders will not be able to finance their building operations.

Since housing is heavily financed by credit, speculation on borrowed money and "thin" equity can lead to overbuilding. In the 1920s a very substantial boom in the construction of apartment houses and office buildings was financed on credit, based on the hope of quick speculative profits. The excess building in that one period depressed the level of such construction for the next 15 years. Moreover, in the past, when a serious economic downturn occurred and mortgage foreclosures became frequent, the lenders who held the mortgages were not anxious to make loans for new construction. Since they already held a large number of residential properties, why should they finance new building in competition with their own holdings?

## Housing in the Postwar Period

Housing construction in the postwar period has behaved somewhat differently from the way it typically did during prewar years. It has been quite high throughout the period, without once falling to the extremely low levels that periodically occurred in the past. And it has fluctuated around these high levels, but with rather quick, sharp cycles, unlike the long-drawn-out booms and depressions before the war.

The rapid population growth in the earlier postwar period and the lack of any major depressions have probably been the most important factors behind the continued high level of home building. Another reason for the continued high volume of construction lies in the government's mortgage guarantee programs. The Federal Housing Administration (FHA) and the Veterans' Administration (VA) insure or guarantee home mortgages and allow these guarantees to be given on mortgages with very low down payments and long maturities. At the same time, in the postwar period there have been large numbers of families earning good incomes, but with little cash for a down payment. These families were willing and able to buy a house with low (or nonexisting) down payments and a long maturity on the mortgage. The FHA and VA programs made such mortgages widely available.

In large part, the shorter cycles in housing construction in the postwar period reflect changing credit conditions. Whenever general economic activity expands rapidly and business firms eagerly seek new loans to finance higher inventories and production, many lenders withdraw funds from the mortgage market and place them in more profitable business loans. They ration their funds to the mortgage market by refusing to lend money on low-down-payment and long-maturity mortgages, confining their loans to the safer ones that have higher down payments and are paid off more quickly. When the general level of interest rates rises, savings and loan associations, which specialize in mortgages, find it difficult to raise correspondingly the interest rates they pay their depositors. Association assets are tied up in earlier mortgages issued at lower interest rates. As a consequence, it becomes increasingly difficult for them to attract new deposits. Potential depositors do not place their savings into savings and loan associations, and some existing deposits are withdrawn, as people seek to take advantage of higher interest rates elsewhere.

For all these reasons, a period of tight money and rising interest rates has a particularly sharp effect on the supply of mortgage funds, driving up mortgage interest rates and restricting mortgage terms. Under these circumstances, many who are in the market for new housing have to withdraw when they find they cannot get low-cost, low-down-payment loans. Builders dependent on credit for their construction funds also find it harder to borrow money, and consequently they cut back their construction activity.

During the moderate recessions, the process reverses itself. Business firms seek fewer loans, releasing funds for mortgages. Interest rates fall, low-down-payment and long-maturity loans are again available, and those potential buyers who have been delaying a home purchase until such easy loans became available re-enter the market. Housing rises swiftly. New housing starts actually rise during recession and fall in expansion despite the contrary income trends, showing the great importance of credit conditions for home building. This countercyclical pattern in residential construction has been an important contribution to the stability of the postwar economy and has acted as an offset to the changes in the other forms of investment.

1968 and 1969 were years of high interest rates and tight money. Yet new housing starts up until the fall of 1969 remained surprisingly high, fluctuating around an annual level of 1.5 million. Did this imply that high interest rates were having no effect on housing construction? Clearly not. In 1968 and 1969 consumer income was high and rising. The number of new families increased sharply during these years, reflecting the huge increase in birth rates that took place at the end of World War II. Under these conditions, the annual number of new housing starts would probably have approached the 2 million level had interest rates been lower and the supply of mortgage credit more plentiful. In other words, the high interest rates of 1968 and 1969, which reflected in part the government's efforts to restrict aggregate demand and control inflation, did significantly reduce housing construction from the level that otherwise would have occurred, even though an actual reduction in housing starts did not occur until late in 1969.

## SUMMARY

The level of GNP, as we saw in Chapter 3, depends on the consumption function on the one hand, and the level of investment and government spending on the other. Changes in investment and government spending have a multiple impact on GNP, as initial changes in spending and income induce further changes through the consumption–GNP relation. Most of the recessions and major depressions of our economic history have been associated with fluctuations in investment spending. We have attempted, therefore, to investigate the major factors determining investment and to discover the reasons for its volatility.

Investment by business firms in *plant and equipment* has a number of characteristics that subject it to wide fluctuations. Purchases of plant and equipment to expand existing facilities depend on the speed with which business sales are changing. Such investment is consequently very sensitive to the *rate of change in GNP*; in particular, this means that investment spending may decline simply because the rate of increase in GNP has slowed down. Another part of investment is associated with the introduction of new techniques and the exploitation of new markets. Such investment often comes in bursts as major new opportunities appear. Changes in investment are also influenced by changes in business profits, which form a major source of funds for financing investment.

On the other hand, these destabilizing features of investment spending are partly dampened by other factors. Actual investment often tends to lag behind the opening up of new investment opportunities: (1) It takes time to order, produce, and install new plant and equipment. (2) Since businessmen are wary of committing themselves to new capacity on the basis of merely temporary increases in their sales, the expansion of facilities often lags behind the rise in sales. (3) There is a limit to how fast the typical business firm can efficiently absorb additions to its plant and equipment. (4) Limitations on the availability of internal funds may force business firms increasingly to borrow for expansion purposes, paying the high interest rates normal during prosperous times. As a consequence, during a period of prosperity a backlog of unexploited investment opportunities often arises, which moderates the decline in investment during a subsequent downturn in sales and profits. However, if the downturn is initially very severe or prolonged, the backlog may disappear, with a consequent very sharp decline in investment spending and a further sharp fall in economic activity.

Businessmen invest in *inventories* as well as in fixed assets. In general, as sales expand, inventories rise, and vice versa. The faster the rise in sales, the greater the desire of business firms to expand inventories. This means that when economic activity is increasing most rapidly, desired investment in inventories will tend to be largest; but when the rate of increase in GNP becomes smaller, inventory investment will decline and become negative. Thus inventory investment is quite sensitive to the rate of change in GNP. Indeed, in minor recessions the largest part of the fluctuation in GNP stems from changes in inventory investment.

*Residential construction* tends to fluctuate more sharply than does the underlying demand for housing. Because of the nature of the housing market, a rise in the demand for housing often leads to an overexpansion of home building that continues well after the increase in demand has subsided. When residential construction finally turns down, therefore, it often remains at a low level for some time, as the population slowly grows into the overbuilt housing stock. In the years before World War II, these characteristics of residential construction led to very long cycles in home construction. The interest cost and availability of credit generally play a large role in determining the level of residential construction activity than they do for other forms of investment. So far in the postwar period, construction has remained high, reflecting the fairly steady growth in disposable income, the absence of any major decline in income, and the rapid growth in population. Relatively sharp, but short-lived, fluctuations around the high level have occurred, reflecting principally changes in credit conditions.

# Money, Prices,

# and Inflation

## CHAPTER FIVE.

So far we have paid little attention to prices. In our discussions of the factors that determine the level of GNP we have tacitly assumed that the general level of prices would remain stable when GNP increased, up to the point of full-employment potential, and that if aggregate demand exceeded potential GNP, prices would begin to rise.

The general price level always rises rapidly during wartime and during most peacetime booms, when total spending is pressing against the full-employment potential. But prices sometimes rise when the economy is operating below full employment. It is time that we looked more carefully at the factors that cause the price level to change. We all want stable prices—but how do we achieve this goal? Is price stability consistent with full employment and rapid economic growth? Who is hurt and who is benefited by inflation? Does a gradual rise in prices over a number of years have serious economic consequences? What about a rapid and sustained inflation? These are the questions we shall examine in this chapter.

## THE GENERAL PRICE LEVEL

In a market economy the movement of individual prices signals to producers the need and desires of buyers. There are literally hundreds of thousands of individual prices for different goods and services. In any period of time, some are rising and others falling. Yet we talk of the desirability of price stability; economic policy tries to prevent either an inflation or deflation of prices. Clearly price stability must refer to the stability of an average of prices around which individual prices fluctuate. It is only in terms of price averages that such terms as "inflation," "deflation," and "price stability" have meaning.

## PRICE INDEXES

There are three major price averages, or more properly *price indexes*, currently in use. The *consumer price index* measures changes in prices of goods and services purchased by moderate-income families. It is an average of prices for about 300 representative items, collected regularly by the Bureau of Labor Statistics. In calculating the index, the price of each item is weighted by its importance in a typical moderate-income family's budget. The *wholesale price index* measures price changes in primary markets—i.e., prices charged by manufacturers and wholesalers. About 2,200 representative commodities are included in this index today. Wholesale price indexes are available for periods as early as the eighteenth century although, needless to say, the price record of very few items goes back so far. A third major index, the *GNP deflator*, is the index used to "deflate" GNP so that it can be measured in real terms, i.e., in "constant prices."

Price indexes are expressed as a percentage of some base period. The consumer and wholesale price indexes are currently published with the base of 1957–1959. In 1969 the consumer price index was 127.7, which means that consumer prices were 27.7 per cent above their average of the years 1957 through 1959. A price index is a weighted average of individual prices. The weights are usually fixed for a number of years and reflect the magnitude of the purchases of the items in the index during the base period.

## SOME SHORTCOMINGS OF PRICE INDEXES

A price index cannot be a perfect measure of the price level; it can only be an approximation. In using price indexes you should keep their limitations in mind.

The longer the time period over which prices are compared, the more questionable the comparison becomes. As incomes and tastes change over the years, buying patterns also change. In 1969, for example, the American consumer spent less of his food dollar on potatoes and bread, and more on fruits and meat, than he did in 1900. In comparing the over-all level of consumer prices between 1900 and 1969, do we use the relative importance of each of these commodities as they were in 1900 or as they were in 1969? It makes a difference to the movement of the over-all index which weights we use. The greater the weights we place

109

on items whose prices have risen the most, the greater will be the rise in the index, and vice versa. Even in a period as short as a decade, consumer buying patterns can shift significantly, thereby changing the weights applied to individual prices. In 1964 the Bureau of Labor Statistics introduced into its consumer price index new weights based on a survey of consumer expenditure patterns in 1961, replacing the weights of a survey of 1951. The importance of food dropped from 28 per cent to 22 per cent in just 10 years.

Price indexes cannot fully measure the changes in the *quality* of goods we buy. Many items that now enter the consumer price index hardly existed in 1900 —automobiles, air conditioners, and frozen food, for example. Even over shorter periods, the quality of many goods changes substantially. When I pay more for a 1971 automobile than I had to pay for a 1948 model, how much of the increase is really a price increase and how much reflects the fact that I am buying an improved car? The statisticians who construct the indexes make adjustments for some of the major measurable quality changes. But many observers feel that there is an upward bias in the price indexes because, on balance, the quality of goods we buy has been gradually improving. What the index counts as a higher price may simply show that we are paying more for a better product—and thus it isn't really a price increase. In the short run, changes in quality are not important enough to overshadow the basic story told by the indexes. But over very long periods of time the "quality problem" is very significant.


## HOW PRICES HAVE CHANGED

Figure 5–1 shows the movement of wholesale prices over the last century and a half. During each war prices shot up rapidly, and then fell off again —with one exception. The price level after World War II, far from declining, continued to rise.

If you look carefully at the chart and ignore the sharp peaks caused by war, it turns out that the nineteenth century was a century of declining prices. Prices at the end of the century were lower than at the beginning. The twentieth century, on the other hand, has been one of rising prices. Prices rose fairly steadily from 1896 to the beginning of World War I. The sharp price decline after that war still left prices in the 1920s well above their prewar level. And even in the Great Depression of the 1930s prices did not fall to the low level they had reached during the major depression of the 1890s. During World War II prices and wages were restrained by price controls much more successfully than they had been in earlier wars. But immediately after the war, instead of falling as they had done in the past, prices rose steeply.

One major difference distinguishing the post–World War II period from other postwar periods is the absence of major depression. The price decline after

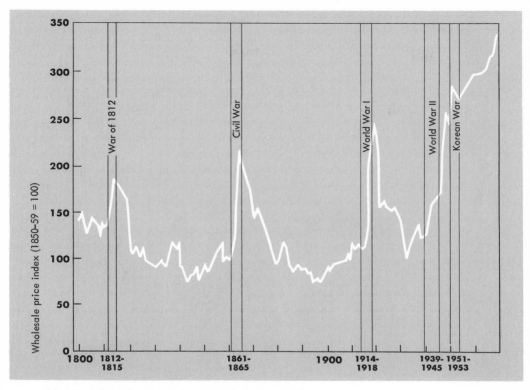

**FIG. 5–1**  Wholesale prices in the United States since 1800

World War I, for example, came during the short, but sharp, depression of 1921, and prices fell again during the depression of 1929–1933. Another important fact to remember in comparing the price increases of the twentieth century with the price behavior of the nineteenth century is the decreasing share of agriculture in total national production. Even as late as 1870 agriculture accounted for about 30 per cent of national production; by the 1920s the proportion had fallen to about 10 per cent, and today the figure is down to 5 per cent. Unlike prices of many manufactured products and most services, agricultural prices are very sensitive even to small declines in the demand for farm products. In an economy in which agriculture accounts for an important share of total output, relatively mild recessions can bring about a decline in the over-all price indexes. But where most prices are fairly insensitive to moderate declines in business activity, significant decreases in over-all price indexes are unlikely to occur in the absence of major depression.

Figures 5–2 and 5–3 give a quick summary of what has happened in recent years to some of the major groups of prices. Since the end of World War II, there

111

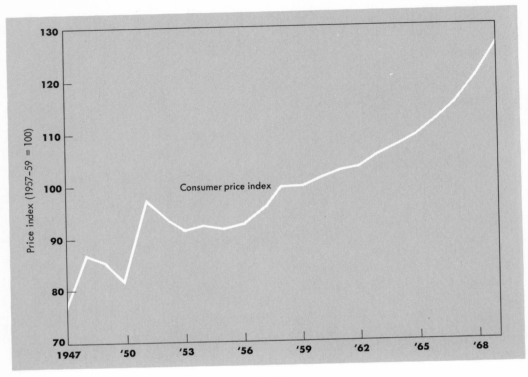

FIG. 5–2    Consumer price index, 1947–1969

have been three periods of major price increases. Immediately after price controls were lifted in 1946, prices rose swiftly until about the middle of 1948. After a slight decline during the recession of 1949, they again rose sharply during the early part of the Korean War in 1950 and 1951. They were relatively stable for the next four years, but rose again, more gradually this time, in 1956 and 1957. Wholesale prices were virtually level from 1958 to 1964, although consumer prices inched up each year. In 1965, wholesale prices began to rise again and the growth of consumer prices accelerated. By the first half of 1970, consumer prices were rising at an annual rate of 6 per cent.

Each of the first two periods of price increase accompanied a large increase in aggregate spending. The first was the postwar buying spree, in which consumers and business firms, flush with cash earned during World War II, were replenishing their depleted stocks. The second was occasioned by the "scare" buying that followed the outbreak of the Korean War, when almost everyone thought that the strict rationing and price controls of World War II were about to be reimposed. In each of these two periods the inflation in prices is fairly easily

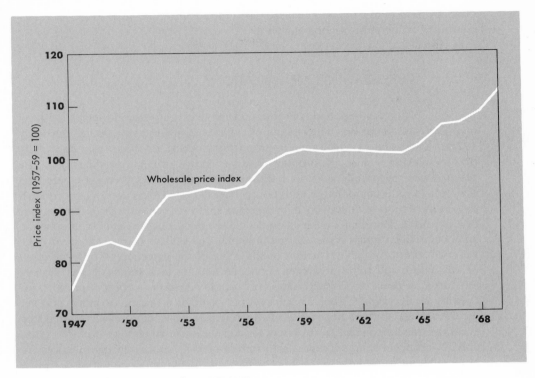

**FIG. 5–3**  Wholesale price index, 1947–1969

explained by the excess of spending relative to the supply of goods available. Or, to put it in terms of our earlier discussions, $C + I + G$ was too high relative to the economy's full-employment potential.

The third period of price rises, starting in late 1955 and ending in early 1958, is harder to explain. Although economic conditions were good, actual GNP during most of the period was not pressing its potential. There were shortages of goods in a few sectors of the economy, but there were surpluses in others. The simple notion that the general level of prices will rise only when there is an overall excess of spending relative to potential GNP does not explain the 1955–1958 price rise very satisfactorily. We shall want to return to this problem later on.

The latest spurt of price increases stemmed originally from the sharp rise in aggregate demand brought about by military spending on the war in Vietnam. Although government spending rose rapidly after U.S. combat troops were sent to Vietnam in 1965, a substantial tax increase was not enacted until the middle of 1968. In the intervening period, aggregate demand had forged ahead of potential GNP, and price rises had become general. Although the combination of a

113

tax increase and tight money had brought aggregate demand below potential GNP by late 1969, inflation proved very intractable and large price increases continued well into the second half of 1970.

## THE MEANING OF INFLATION

The term *inflation* is ordinarily used to mean a rise in the general level of prices. But there are many kinds of inflation. In Germany during the early 1920s an inflation of truly gigantic proportions occurred. Prices rose so rapidly that they began to lose all meaning. Postage stamps originally selling for a few pennies were eventually sold for billions of German marks. Workers, receiving their pay, would immediately rush for the store, since prices were changed each day. Failure to shop on payday might mean a sharp reduction in the buying power of a paycheck. Running a business under these conditions was almost impossible, and conducting foreign trade was unthinkable. The savings of rich and poor alike were wiped out by the destruction of the value of the currency. A *hyperinflation* of this nature will bring organized economic activity to a standstill and destroy the currency itself. In some countries of South America, however, prices have risen by an average of 10 to 20 per cent per year for a decade or more, and yet the economies continue to function. Economic activity is, of course, distorted, for everyone tries to conduct his business to reap the most advantage from the inflation. Investments having the greatest promise of high returns during inflation are often different from those that would be most profitable under conditions of price stability—real estate speculation, for example, is a favorite object of investment in many of these countries.

Except during time of war, price increases in the United States have been fairly modest. The kind of major distortions in economic activity that accompany a rapid inflation have generally been absent. Nevertheless, even a modest annual increase in prices, if continued over many years, adds up to a significant loss in the value of the dollar. For example, if prices rose at an average of 3 per cent per year, it would take only 14 years for the price level to rise 50 per cent. To those living on fixed incomes, or drawing on past savings held in savings accounts or bonds, a 50 per cent price rise would involve a substantial reduction in living standards.

Who gains and who loses by inflation depends to some extent on the nature of the phenomenon. Typically, however, the debtor will gain, since the real value of his debt is reduced by the price increase. The creditor, repaid in money that has less purchasing power than the monies he lent, will lose. In the nineteenth century, one of the major political divisions was between the debtor-farmer of the Midwest, who wanted "cheap money" and an end to falling prices, and the "hard money" Eastern creditors, who stood to gain as long as prices fell. It was this split that gave rise to the famous "cross of gold" speech of William Jennings Bryan, who championed the easy-money interests of the farmers.

114

The risk taker and the speculator will generally gain during an inflation; the conservative investor will tend to lose. The worker in an industry whose sales are booming may well come out ahead in inflation. His salaried neighbor may lose. Older people living on a fixed income make out poorly in inflation, whereas younger people are more likely to profit. Inflation redistributes income in a more or less arbitrary manner, and the more violent the inflation, the more drastic the income redistribution.

The differences between the ruinous inflation of Germany in the 1920s, the steady 10 to 20 per cent a year inflation in some South American countries, and the modest price increase that our own economy has experienced, are so great that one might wonder about using the same term to describe all these conditions. Nevertheless, let us define inflation simply as a rise in the general price level. But let us remember that the effect of inflation on an economy will vary tremendously, depending on how rapid it is.

## CHANGES IN RELATIVE PRICES AND IN THE PRICE LEVEL

A rise in the general price level is quite a different thing from a rise in prices of particular commodities. In a market economy changes in individual prices, both up and down, perform an essential function in directing production toward the needs and desires of consumers. Suppose, for example, there is a change in consumer tastes from canned food to frozen food. At first, the demand for frozen food will exceed the supply. Prices of frozen food will tend to rise, profits in the industry will increase, and plant and equipment will be expanded. It will be necessary to hire more workers in frozen-food plants, and wages might have to be increased to attract the additional labor force. With heavier supplies of frozen foods coming on the market, the gap between demand and supply will be reduced, and eventually eliminated. The opposite process will have been occurring in the canned-food industry, and the excess of supply over demand will tend to be wiped out. In this way, resources are shifted about to match changes in consumer demands. — rise in price of particular commodity

A rise in the general price level, unlike changes in particular prices, performs no beneficial economic function. In the first place, when *total* spending is excessive relative to potential GNP, there are no additional resources to call on. In the frozen food–canned food example above, a price increase for one commodity, accompanied by a price decrease for another, shifted resources in the direction preferred by consumers. But a rise in the general price level does not redirect resources. Moreover, when there is an excess of demand relative to the supply of a particular commodity, a rise in price tends to eliminate the excess, both by encouraging an increase in supply and discouraging some of the demand. But this is not true of an increase in the general price level. Every price is also an income. For example, the $3,000 I pay for an automobile becomes $3,000 worth

general price level increase

115

of profits and wages to the auto industry. If the price rose to $3,200, then my purchase would involve $3,200 of profit and wage income to the auto industry. When the general price level rises, therefore, money incomes throughout the economy will also tend to rise. If prices rose while money incomes remained unchanged, then indeed a rise in the general price level would carry with it the seeds of its own destruction. With a fixed total of money incomes, higher prices would mean that less could be purchased and the initial excess spending that initiated the price increase would be wiped out. But since higher prices all around lead to higher wages and profits, and therefore higher money incomes, an increase in the general price level does not directly reduce spending.

## THE WAGE–PRICE SPIRAL

When spending is excessive relative to potential GNP, unemployment will be quite low and labor scarce. Businessmen will be actively seeking additional workers in order to increase their production, and wages will rise rapidly. The excess demand will lead, therefore, to both higher prices and higher wages. In some cases prices will lead the procession, as businessmen raise their markups to take advantage of the favorable market. There may be other industries, however, whose sales have not shared in the boom, where the general shortage of labor nevertheless leads to wage increases and only thereafter to a price increase based on the higher cost of production. These wage and price increases tend to reinforce each other. As we pointed out in the preceding paragraph, higher wages generate additional money income and stimulate spending. Moreover, the higher wage costs will lead to still further price increases. In turn, the rising cost of living will be reflected in further wage demands, as unions attempt to keep up with the inflation. Finally, to the extent that the experience of *actual* price increases generates expectations of future price increases, additional fuel is added to the inflationary engine. If prices are expected to rise tomorrow, everyone will want to make his purchases today. Saving is discouraged, spending encouraged. The $C + I + G$ curve shifts upward, and the excess of demand over supply is increased still further. Fortunately, however, it does not appear that a very mild inflation of 1 or 2 per cent per year is enough to generate this kind of self-feeding, cumulative reaction. It apparently takes a more violent price rise to set off such a chain of expectations.

In summary, an inflation has some of the properties of a perpetual motion machine. An excessive aggregate demand for goods and labor leads to a rise in prices, wages, and profits. On the other hand, the rise in wages and profits offsets the effect of rising prices on consumer buying power so that, for the economy as a whole, aggregate real purchasing power is not reduced, and the initial excess spending is perpetuated. At the same time, the higher wages lead to higher costs of production and still higher prices. In turn, a rising cost of living adds new fuel to the demand for still higher wages. Thus wages chase prices and prices chase wages. In this process, of course, not everybody fares equally. Demand may not be excessive in all industries. Some business firms experiencing little rise in the demand for their product will nevertheless have to pay higher wages; their profits may actually be reduced. With other firms the opposite will occur; their demand will be so strong that they can raise prices by more than their increase in costs. Some workers, whose services are in particularly high demand or whose union is particularly strong, may beat the inflation, as their wages rise faster than prices; other groups of workers will lag substantially behind. It is because of factors like this that in countries where rapid inflation has occurred, stabilization measures are extremely difficult to adopt. Attempting to halt the process in midstream will always penalize those groups that have not caught up with the inflation. Yet, allowing their incomes to rise enough to catch up may so increase spending as to start the whole process all over again.

## MONEY AND INFLATION

Although in many of its aspects inflation can be a self-perpetuating spiral, there are certain built-in obstacles to such a process. The first of these has to do primarily with money. Without an increase in the supply of money, no major inflation can last very long.[1]

Since almost all transactions in our economy are carried on with money, and since receipts and expenditures usually do not occur simultaneously, individuals and business firms must hold a supply of money. The business firm has an inflow of receipts from sales and an outflow of payments to workers and suppliers. Since receipts and expenditures do not occur simultaneously, the firm must keep a reserve of money on hand. If, for example, it wants to increase its output, the firm must buy additional raw materials and meet increased payrolls before it obtains added revenue from the higher level of output.

As a consequence, when prices, wages, and output rise, business needs for money will increase.[2] *As a general rule, the greater the volume of monetary transactions in the economy, the higher the level of money required to finance the transactions*. When GNP rises, therefore, "transactions requirements" for money will also rise.

When the general price level rises, the value of GNP in money terms increases. Even though output and employment may not increase (since the econ-

---

[1] James Duesenberry's *Money and Credit: Impact and Control*, 2nd ed., another volume in this Series, examines the monetary system in detail. Our discussion will, therefore, be kept very brief.

[2] The firm might purchase its materials on credit from its suppliers, but this simply shifts the need for money to another firm.

omy is already at full employment), higher prices and wages mean increased business receipts, payrolls, and raw-materials purchases. As a consequence, the need for money to meet transactions requirements increases. But with the total supply of money in the economy unchanged, business firms, state and local governments, home buyers, and others have to compete with one another to obtain their growing needs out of a constant money supply. To some extent in the economy, there may be "idle" cash that is being held over and above minimum transactions needs and can be enticed back into circulation through the payment of attractive interest rates; and business firms can, to a degree, economize on their use of cash. Nevertheless, a "tight money" situation will develop.

As the inflation proceeds, the increased demands for money will press ever harder on the limited supply. With borrowers competing for the scarce supply of cash, interest rates (the price for the use of money) will tend to rise, and credit will become more difficult to obtain on favorable terms. Lenders will begin to screen out the riskier loans. Some home buyers, finding that mortgages on easy terms (no down payment, 30 years to pay) can no longer be obtained, will be forced to postpone their purchases. State and local governments will see the interest cost of their borrowing increase, and some will decide to wait a while before proceeding with the new school or the new waste-treatment plant. Some business firms, particularly those that have to borrow a large part of their investment funds, will decide to scale down their investment plans because of the higher cost of borrowing. All these developments will cause a reduction in spending; the $C + I + G$ curve will begin shifting *downward*. Eventually a new equilibrium will be reached. The excess spending will be eliminated and prices will stop rising. Prices will, however, tend to remain at the higher level, unless some new inflationary or deflationary force comes along.

All *major* inflations must be fed by an increase in the supply of money. If the monetary authorities keep the money supply from rising, the resulting scarcity of money, tightening of credit, and increases in interest rates will eventually halt an inflation. But this does not mean that there is any neat one-to-one relationship between the money supply and prices. Occasionally in the popular press, or in speeches by businessmen and bankers, the term "inflation" is used synonymously with increases in the money supply; any rise in the money supply is termed "inflationary." But in actuality, the connection between money and prices is quite complex. Money does not affect prices directly in some mysterious way, but only through its influence on spending. Spending, in turn, can rise by moderate amounts even when the money supply is constant, as individuals and business firms economize on their cash and as pockets of "idle" cash balances are drawn into circulation. There is a limit, however, to how far spending can increase without a rise in the money supply. Finally, in discussing the relation between money and prices, we must not forget that a rise in spending need not result in rising prices when the economy is operating with idle resources, well below full-employment levels.

## FOREIGN TRADE AND INFLATION

In addition to the money supply, there are other factors that may tend to limit the self-perpetuating nature of the inflationary process. If the inflation is not world wide, rising prices will tend to discourage exports and encourage imports. This will reduce excess demand in the exporting country; demand for its exports will decline, and more of its own spending will go for imports. With more of aggregate demand being met out of foreign production and the demand for exports declining, income payments diminish, reducing the succeeding rounds of spending. Of course, after a point, the inflating country may offset the rising prices for its exports by devaluing its currency relative to other currencies.[3] So long as exchange rates are fixed, however, an inflation in one country brought on by excess spending will be tempered by the depressing effect of price increases on its foreign trade.

## TAXES AND FISCAL POLICY

A progressive tax system will also tend to slow down inflation. Under a progressive tax, higher incomes are subject to a higher tax rate. When money incomes rise during an inflation, therefore, the percentage of total income taken in taxes will automatically increase, and private spending will be reduced. (This assumes, of course, that the government does not increase its spending as rapidly as its revenues increase.)

The government can also pursue a deliberately anti-inflationary fiscal policy. Suppose, for example, that an investment boom raises total spending above productive capacity. By reducing its own expenditures, or by raising tax rates, the government can depress the $C + I + G$ curves to the point where aggregate spending is again equal to full-employment potential, and the excess spending disappears. During a war, government spending itself may be the chief cause for pushing the $C + I + G$ curves up above capacity. Theoretically, fiscal policy could handle the situation by a massive offsetting increase in taxes. In practice, however, none of our major wars have been completely tax-financed, although taxes were raised substantially. It has always been felt, rightly or wrongly, that too large a tax increase might impede the war effort. Direct price controls and rationing were used, particularly in World War II, to hold down prices and wages and to keep the wage–price spiral from getting out of hand. The result was "repressed inflation"; total demand remained excessive, but the price and wage

[3]Suppose, for example, that 10 units of country A's currency are exchanged for 1 U.S. dollar. If country A's export prices doubled, then a U.S. importer could buy only half as much for a dollar as he could before the inflation started. If, however, country A devalued, so that its currency exchanged at a rate of 20 units to the dollar, its export prices in terms of U.S. dollars would be back to where they were before the inflation started.

consequences were avoided—or at least postponed until after the war—by direct controls.

One of the major objectives of fiscal policy is to *prevent* excess spending in the first place. Once prices have risen, it is very painful and generally undesirable to reduce them again. Reducing prices would require that spending be held *below* the full-employment potential in order to create enough unemployment and excess plant capacity to force wage and price cuts. No modern government is likely to adopt this policy. Once prices have risen, so long as the increases do not continue, the economy fairly well adapts itself to the new price level. The benefits, if any, from returning to the lower price level would be small compared to the political and economic costs of heavy unemployment and idle factories, and the risk that a major depression might be set in motion. The primary goal of anti-inflation policy in modern economies is to stop the rise in prices, not to reduce prices to their earlier level.

## OTHER KINDS OF INFLATION

### Cost–Push

So far we have discussed inflation as if it arose solely from excessive aggregate demand. Many economists believe, however, that inflation can also occur in periods when demand is not excessive, because of wage increases that exceed productivity gains.[4] Much of the inflation of the 1950s, they believe, stemmed not so much from excess demand "pulling" up prices, but from cost increases that "pushed" up prices.

The period from 1955 through early 1958 seemed to confirm this view. There were few signs of excess aggregate demand after late 1955. Although sales of machinery and equipment were booming, sales of automobiles, appliances, and housing were disappointingly low. Plant capacity was plentiful, and unemployment never fell below 4 per cent of the labor force. Yet consumer and wholesale prices rose about 3 per cent per year during the period. Wages and salaries

[4] It is only wage increases *in excess of* productivity increases that bring about a rise in costs. If, for example, hourly wages rise 3 per cent per year and output per man-hour worked also rises 3 per cent, then labor costs per unit of production remain unchanged. For example:

|  |  |  |
|---|---|---|
| Year 1 | Output | 100 units |
|  | Man-hours required | 100 man-hours |
|  | Payroll at $2.00 per hour | 200 dollars |
|  | Labor cost per unit produced | 2 dollars |
| Year 2 | Output | 100 units |
|  | Man-hours required (3% productivity increase) | 97 man-hours (rounded) |
|  | Payroll at $2.06 per hour (3% wage increase) | 200 dollars |
|  | Labor cost per unit produced | 2 dollars |

rose much faster than productivity, and even though prices also rose, profit margins were narrowed. But the wage gains occurred in nonunion as well as union plants, and salaries rose as fast—if not faster—than wages. There were particularly sharp price and wage increases in the steel industry, which were in turn reflected in higher prices in a number of steel-using products, even where demand was not excessive. The straight "classical" explanation of inflation, as the result of an excess aggregate demand, hardly appears to fit the 1955–1958 period.

On closer examination, however, it is not easy to distinguish *demand–pull* from *cost–push* inflation. As we discussed earlier, when spending is pressing on full-employment capacity, labor is scarce and wages are bid up faster than productivity is increasing. Indeed, this is what keeps a demand–pull inflation going; higher wages mean higher income and additional spending. Even when the basic cause of inflation is excessive spending, many businessmen first see the inflation as a rise in wages they have to pay. The important distinction between demand–pull and cost–push inflation, therefore, is not between a situation in which wage costs rise and one in which they do not. Costs rise in all inflations. Rather, the major question to ask is whether costs and prices rise *in the absence of an excess demand for goods and labor.* If they do, then we may have cost–push inflation.

Many of our most important industries are dominated by a few large firms and one or a few powerful unions. Both management and labor in these industries do take market conditions into account in formulating their wage and price policies. There is, however, evidence from the postwar period that wage bargains tend to exceed productivity gains even when unemployment is higher than the 3 or 4 per cent we generally associate with full employment. And the resulting cost increases are often fully passed on, in some cases with an added markup, even in the face of substantial excess capacity in the industry. In essence, the problem is not that cost–push inflation is insensitive to the level of aggregate demand. There is *some* level of unemployment and excess plant capacity that will keep increases in wages from exceeding average productivity gains and prevent profit margins from being raised. What worries many economists is that prices and wages may start to creep up even when GNP is below its potential and unemployment and excess capacity are too high.

### Sector Inflation

Even in periods when aggregate demand in the economy as a whole is not excessive relative to the nation's potential, some industries will be enjoying a boom while others experience a decline in sales and orders. If our price system worked perfectly, prices would rise in industries with excessive demand and fall in industries with slack demand. Resources of manpower, materials, and capital would flow into the booming industries and out of the declining industries. But so long as demand *in the aggregate* was not excessive, the price increases and decreases would balance each other, and the general price level would not rise. As a matter of fact, however, prices in the modern industrial economy are more likely to rise when demand is excessive than to fall when demand is slack. Prices tend to be rigid downward—they do not fall easily. This is bound to impart an upward bias to the over-all price level.

The inflation that occurred in 1955–1958 resulted, in part at least, from this kind of behavior. During this period new orders and sales of machinery and equipment rose substantially and prices of these items increased sharply. At the same time, during all but the early part of this period, the demand for automobiles and housing declined fairly steeply. Yet prices of housing and automobiles also rose, though less sharply than machinery prices. Wages in industries whose markets were declining increased at about the same rate as wages in industries with booming sales. If prices increase when demand is high and do not fall when demand falls, and if wages in booming industries become the model for wages elsewhere, then the general price level will surely rise.

Downward rigidity of prices tends to encourage an upward creep in the price level in yet another way. Although average productivity in the economy has been rising some 3 per cent a year, productivity gains in a number of important industries often exceed these average gains. If their prices are not reduced, profit margins in such industries will rise rapidly. Unions will not stand by idly and see these profits accumulate; they will press vigorously for large wage increases. And if the rapid gains in productivity are accompanied by large increases in industry sales, they will succeed in their attempts. A number of recent statistical investigations have found that the magnitude of profits is a key element in determining the size of wage increases. Industries where productivity is rising very sharply may be able to afford substantial wage increases without increasing prices. But the abnormally large wage increases will become targets for other unions in industries where productivity increases are less rapid. And to the extent that such wage patterns are followed, prices in these industries will have to rise.

In short, above-average productivity gains in particular industries will eventually result in either price reductions or large profits which may lead to large wage increases. If prices are not reduced and large wage increases occur, this will, in all likelihood, soon be reflected in wage and price increases in industries with average or below-average productivity gains. Paradoxically, therefore, the failure of some prices to fall can cause other prices to rise.

## FULL EMPLOYMENT
## AND PRICE STABILITY

It is generally agreed that the inflations that accompanied World War II and the Korean War were chiefly demand–pull inflations, in which the main culprit was excessive aggregate demand. If the over-all price level rose *only* when demand was excessive relative to full-employment GNP, there would be a relatively simple solution. Appropriate changes in federal expenditures and taxes could eliminate any inflationary spending gap and at the same time keep the economy at full employment by shifting the $C + I + G$ curves to the point where total spending would be neither excessive nor deficient. The line $(C + I + G)_0$ in Fig. 5–4 represents the objective of such a policy. If an inflationary gap should exist, represented by the aggregate demand schedule $(C + I + G)_2$, increases in federal taxes could shift aggregate demand down (higher taxes reduce disposable income and lower the consumption–GNP relation). Or, with taxes unchanged, a decrease in federal expenditures could reduce the aggregate demand curve. Should the situation be one of a deflationary gap and unemployment represented by the aggregate demand schedule $(C + I + G)_1$, an appropriate fiscal response would, of course, be just the reverse; taxes should be reduced or expenditures increased, in order to shift the aggregate demand schedule back up toward the $(C + I + G)_0$ position. (Monetary policy, by affecting the ease or tightness of credit, can also cause the spending curves, particularly investment spending, to shift in the desired direction.) Of course, fiscal and monetary policy do not work perfectly, and errors on either side would undoubtedly occur. Nevertheless, there would be no conflict between the goals of full employment and price stability, even though we might not reach perfection in achieving them.

From the experience of the 1950s and 1960s, however, we have learned that matters are not quite that simple. There is some evidence of a mild upward bias in prices and wages *such that the general price level begins to rise before full*

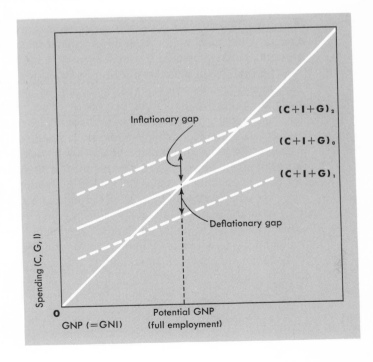

**FIG. 5–4** Full employment and price stability through fiscal and monetary policy

*employment is reached.* Prices will remain stable only if spending is held below the full-employment level. Striving for maximum full employment at all times would probably result in a slow inflation. On the other hand, fixing our sights solely on price stability would force on us an undesirably high level of unemployment and excess capacity, and probably reduce our rate of economic growth. In economics, as in most other areas of life, there are often no easy solutions. When two goals are incompatible, we have to compromise between them, while continuing to seek new methods of achieving both.

In trying to secure both full employment and a reasonably stable price level, one of the secrets of success apparently is to halt incipient inflation quickly, before it gets a good start. During recent years (1965–1970), we have seen how difficult it is to halt an inflation by gradual means. The inflation that accompanied the Vietnam war started in late 1965, slacked off for a while in 1967, and resumed again in 1968. But, as we pointed out earlier, taxes were not increased as an anti-inflationary device until mid-1968. And even then for the next six months, monetary policy was relatively easy, because the monetary authorities feared that the fiscal policy being pursued might be too drastic. As a consequence inflationary pressures built up a good head of steam. Two kinds of problems tend to arise under these circumstances.

First, if aggregate demand has been rising excessively for some period of time, business firms may begin projecting those increases into the future and base their investment plans on inflationary expectations. $C + I + G$ curves rise still more, and very restrictive monetary and fiscal policies may be needed to offset such expectations. But once the expectations have been reversed by stringent monetary and fiscal policy, aggregate demand may drop quite sharply, leading to substantial unemployment.

Second, when inflation has been under way for a long period, there are always many workers whose wages have not yet caught up with the rising cost of living and many business firms that have not yet raised their prices to cover earlier wage increases. As a consequence, even if monetary and fiscal policies should be successful in eliminating the excess demand, so that the $C + I + G$ curves intersect GNP just at full-employment levels, prices and wages may continue to rise for a while in an inflationary manner as these firms and workers catch up. But with aggregate demand restrained in its growth, continued increases in prices and wages may well lead to a fall in output and a rise in unemployment.

In short, once an inflation has been going for a long time, it is difficult for monetary and fiscal policy to "nudge" aggregate demand lower, and likely that price and wage increases will continue for some time after the basic inflationary pressure has disappeared. In seeking to maintain both full employment and price stability, an ounce of prevention is indeed worth a pound of cure.

In late 1968 and throughout 1969 and 1970, the government was attempting to steer a delicate course. It desired to stop inflation. If that had been its only objective, the job would have been easy; it is always possible to adopt a stringent enough set of fiscal and monetary policies to halt inflation in its tracks through a drastic reduction in aggregate demand. But this course would have surely led to a very sharp recession and a large rise in unemployment. For fear of this consesequence, the government was trying to "ease" down gradually the excess aggregate demand, sufficiently to dampen inflationary pressures but not so radically or quickly as to lead to a sharp drop in business activity. We have had no experience in successfully tapering off an inflation without a subsequent recession. Each of the postwar inflations was followed immediately by a recession, with unemployment rates climbing into the 6 and 7 per cent levels. The objectives of the fiscal and monetary authorities were indeed laudable as they tried to halt the inflation gradually, without bringing on a recession. At the time of this writing, it was too early to tell whether they would prove successful.

## MEASURES TO RECONCILE
## FULL EMPLOYMENT AND PRICE STABILITY

To the extent that there is some upward bias in the price level, we need to explore possibilities for making full employment compatible with price stability.

When unemployment is very high, there are many more people looking for work than there are jobs to be filled. An increase in aggregate demand can create job opportunities for the unemployed to fill. And this increase in job opportunities —i.e., in business firms' demand for workers—need not lead to excessive wage increase, because there are many unemployed workers looking for jobs at current wages. But, in the American economy, once unemployment drops to a level of 3.5 to 4 per cent, further increases in job opportunities, through increases in aggregate demand, tend to create an over-all scarcity of labor and lead to wage increases in excess of productivity gains. This is because the 3.5 to 4 per cent of the labor force who remain unemployed generally do not have the skills to match employers' job requirements. On the average, many of the remaining unemployed tend to be those with little education, with few marketable skills, and with residences far removed from where the jobs are. As new job vacancies are created by increases in aggregate demand, they cannot be filled with those currently unemployed. Paradoxically, both job vacancies and unemployed people exist at the same time. Jobs go unfilled and there is a scarcity of labor, even though 3.5 to 4 per cent of the work force are still seeking work. Further increases in aggregate demand do more to raise wages and prices than to reduce unemployment.

One way of meeting this problem is to conduct training programs to give the hard-core unemployed the skills necessary to fit into the job vacancies that exist. By creating a better match between the unemployed and the job vacancies, a two-fold objective can be accomplished: (1) the unemployed and the low-wage

125

worker can be given the opportunity to earn better incomes; and, (2) the inflationary pressure of unfilled job vacancies, which tends to arise when unemployment rates are low, can be reduced. Price stability can be made more compatible with high employment. The large increase in governmentally sponsored manpower training programs in recent years has been a response to both these objectives. Another approach, tried only experimentally so far in the United States, is to give unemployed workers moving allowances and other moving assistance in cases where job vacancies exist in one part of the country and unemployed workers with the necessary skills live in other areas.

Guideposts

In the early 1960s, the government also advanced "Guideposts for Noninflationary Price and Wage Behavior," and urged leaders of business and labor to follow them. The guideposts were spelled out in annual reports of the Council of Economic Advisers to the President.

The general guidepost for wages stated that wages should not rise by more than the economy-wide productivity trend. If all wages followed this principle, labor costs per unit of output would remain constant. The general guidepost for prices called on industries with average productivity gains to keep their prices unchanged; for industries with higher productivity gains to pass the benefit on in lower prices; and for industries with lower productivity gains to raise prices by no more than their increases in unit costs. These general guideposts were qualified by exceptions: industries paying particularly low wages could appropriately give higher increases for the sake of equity; industries could pay more to attract additional labor. Prices could rise beyond the general guideposts if nonlabor costs rose and if an industry was unable to attract capital that it needed. During all this period, the guideposts remained voluntary in nature. Their observance could not be enforced by law—although on some occasions Presidents Kennedy and Johnson denounced particular price or wage increases, thus using the considerable moral force of the presidency to maintain guidepost behavior.

The guideposts probably had some beneficial effects on prices and cost stability by making leaders of business and labor more aware of the impact of their actions on the performance of the economy. Such guideposts are no substitute for proper fiscal and monetary policies that keep aggregate demand within the economy's potential GNP. But they can help modestly to permit fuller utilization of labor and capital without the economy lapsing into inflation.

Once aggregate demand exceeded potential GNP, in late 1965, prices began to rise significantly despite the guideposts. It became more and more difficult to call upon labor to hold its wage demands within the limits of productivity gains once the cost of living had started to rise sharply. Moreover, with labor shortages developing, business firms could more easily grant large wage increases, painlessly passing the higher costs along in a booming market (in some cases with an added markup). Specific guidepost criteria were abandoned, although general calls for restraint in wage and price action were sporadically issued by the government. Once an inflation had got under way, it proved to be very difficult to formulate a specific set of guideposts with even a modest chance of being accepted by business and labor. In its early days, the Nixon administration explicitly renounced the use of "moral suasion" and guidepost principles as means of restraining inflation.

To the extent that guideposts are useful, they are undoubtedly more effective in *maintaining* price stability during a full-employment period than in *restoring* price stability once inflation has started. It is entirely possible, however, that once inflationary excess aggregate demand has been eliminated, through fiscal and monetary actions, some kind of guidepost criteria might again be useful as a means of phasing down the rate of wage and price increases faster than would happen if natural forces were left to work their will.

A number of European countries have adopted similar measures, called "incomes policies." These policies are based on the theory that inflation is caused by an excess of income claims (in the form of wages, profits, etc.) over the economy's real ability to meet these claims. If incomes are too high compared to production, inflation results; the problem is to limit the rise of incomes to the rise in real production.

European experience with these policies has been very mixed. Sometimes unions have refused to limit their claims to the productivity advance. And where the central union leaders were "reasonable" and "responsible," local conditions have sometimes led to "wage drift," a rise of actual wage payments beyond the terms specified in the nationally negotiated wage contracts. The experience suggests that "incomes policies" (or "guideposts") cannot undo the damage of general excess demand, though there is a useful role for them under conditions of balanced growth of aggregate demand and potential GNP.

We should also search for other ways to reduce any inflationary bias of the economy. Are there other methods of preventing a disastrous collapse in farm income besides pegging farm prices at a high level? We might also take a hard look at our nineteenth-century regulatory policies, which often maintain uneconomically high railroad and truck rates, and the maritime policies that, on vague grounds of national security, heavily subsidize an expensive merchant marine and at the same time permit shipping rates to be pegged by cartel-like shipping "conferences." We may need changed legislation with respect to particular union policies—especially those of certain unions which make entry of new workers into the labor market difficult. It may be that our antitrust laws, or their ways of enforcement, need to be changed to place more emphasis on the importance of price flexibility—downward as well as upward. Both price stability and full employment are too important as economic goals to allow one to prevent the achievement of the other.

## SUMMARY

It is the general price level, not individual prices, that is relevant in discussing inflation and deflation. The three most widely used indicators of the general price level are the *consumer price index*, the *wholesale price index*, and the *GNP deflator*.

Prices generally have risen throughout the twentieth century, but in spurts rather than steadily. During wars, the general price level rises sharply, as aggregate spending presses on capacity. After each war, except World War II, prices fell, although not always back to prewar levels. Since World War II, prices have risen in four major spurts: the postwar reconversion period, the Korean War, the period 1955 through 1958, and the inflation that accompanied the war in Vietnam.

The inflation that arises from excess aggregate demand involves a self-perpetuating wage–price spiral. Higher prices lead to higher wages and higher wages to higher prices. The rising money incomes that go with higher prices and wages keep spending high.

With the money supply held constant, however, an inflationary spiral will eventually be brought to a halt by a scarcity of money, tight credit, and rising interest rates. Major inflation must be fueled by injections of additional money. However, there is no neat one-to-one relationship between money and prices.

Although major inflations arise from excessive demand relative to productive capacity (demand–pull), there is some evidence that prices may begin to rise gradually even when spending is below the full-employment potential. Wage increases in excess of productivity gains push prices up (cost–push). Also, the fact that prices in many large industries rise when demand is high but often do not fall equally when demand is low tends to cause the general price level to rise even if over-all demand is not excessive.

To the extent that there is an upward bias in prices and wages, full employment and price stability may not be simultaneously possible. However, the degree of price inflation that would accompany full employment is probably not very great (assuming demand were not excessive).

The government attempted to reduce the inflationary bias by adopting manpower training policies and, during the early 1960s, by propounding guideposts for noninflationary price and wage behavior. Other countries have adopted similar incomes policies.

# Economic Growth

# in the United States

We have concentrated thus far on the factors that determine the relation between *actual* and *potential* output. Up to the limit set by economic potential, how much the economy actually produces will depend on the level of demand. We have, therefore, devoted our efforts to explaining the forces that determine the demand for goods and services. For economic growth to occur over any substantial period of time, however, potential output—economic capacity, if you will—must increase.

A nation that is producing below its potential can, to be sure, grow for a while merely by pursuing policies that increase demand; as idle workers are re-employed and excess plant capacity is put to use, output will increase. In this case the nation can "grow into" its existing capacity. But once actual output equals potential output, further increases in demand will simply lead to inflation rather than to a growth in real output, unless economic potential itself begins to rise. In other words, the problem of economic fluctuations is primarily a problem of *demand*; long-term economic growth, on the other hand, is chiefly a problem of *supply*—of growth in potential capacity to produce goods and services. This chapter examines the forces that determine the growth in economic potential.

One major *caveat* is in order here. Our discussion of economic growth is confined to advanced industrial countries such as the United States. This chapter deals neither with the problems of economic growth in the less-developed countries of the world nor with the early origins of growth in the United States.[1] Much of what is said in this chapter about

---

[1]These problems are the central topic of Richard T. Gill, *Economic Development: Past and Present*, 2nd ed., another volume in this Series.

economic growth in the United States and about such matters as investment, saving, and technological progress is relevant for an understanding of growth anywhere in the world. Yet, more fundamentally, a very large part of the growth problems in the less-developed nations stems from the difficulties of changing age-old customs, attitudes, and institutions. Much of the framework we take for granted as part of the explanation for economic growth in the United States does not exist in these countries. The reader is therefore warned against an easy transference to the less-developed countries of conclusions that arise out of a discussion of economic growth in the United States.

There are, as a matter of fact, two opposite kinds of fallacies about the growth problems of the less-developed countries, one fully as pernicious as the other. The first is the one mentioned above—the belief that the problem of economic development in these countries can be solved simply through the application of a set of highly specific technical economic principles derived from the experience of the wealthier industrial nations. Its opposite, equally to be avoided, is the belief that growth problems of the less-developed countries are purely political or social in nature, and that there are no general economic principles that provide useful guidance.

## MEASURING POTENTIAL GNP

Since economic growth concerns the rate at which potential GNP is advancing, we ought to start with a careful definition of that term. So far, we have defined potential GNP as the GNP that the economy could produce at a given time under conditions of reasonably full employment and normal utilization of plant capacity. Reasonably full employment does not mean that everyone willing and able to work has a job. Even in a prosperous economy there will be some declining industries that are laying off workers while other industries grow. Automation and other improvements in production destroy some jobs. Under the best of conditions, it takes a while for workers who are being let out of work in the declining industries to find jobs in the expanding ones, or for those affected by labor-saving improvements to relocate. A truly prosperous economy is one in which there are sufficient unfilled job opportunities so that the vast majority of displaced workers who are willing to seek work in other jobs do not have an unreasonable wait before finding employment.

The "frictional" unemployment that is a more or less unavoidable minimum under current conditions in the United States is put by most economists at somewhere between 3 and 4 per cent of the labor force. The adoption of widespread retraining programs, moving allowances for displaced workers, and other programs to increase skills and mobility could reduce this minimum. Many European countries have, in the last 15 years, achieved unemployment rates that have remained at or below 2 per cent without, apparently, putting severe inflationary strains on their economies. Let us, however, be conservative, and define full employment to exist when 96 per cent of the labor force is employed. Remember that the 4 per cent pool of unemployed is not made up of the same people month in and month out. When the economy is at full employment, the majority of the unemployed are only temporarily in that category. During any single period, some workers, just let out of their jobs, are entering the pool of unemployed as others are leaving it to return to work. The workers who are out of work for extended periods of time, when the over-all unemployment rate is at or below 4 per cent, tend to be those with little education and meager job skills. Improvements in education and manpower training programs, rather than a more rapid over-all growth rate, are the answer to the problem of this residual hard-core unemployment.

Given the "96 per cent employed" criterion, we can find the amount of employment corresponding to full employment by multiplying the labor force by 96 per cent. The labor force, in turn, consists of those members of the population who are able and willing to work. The Bureau of the Census conducts a survey each month to determine the number of people in the labor force, and how many of those are employed or unemployed. It asks a series of carefully drawn questions to determine whether a person was employed or actively seeking work.

The size of the labor force is usually somewhat larger during prosperity than during recessions. Under depressed economic conditions, some people, particularly young people and housewives, having been unable to find a job for some months, give up looking and no longer report themselves as seeking work. In a period of labor shortage, extra people are drawn into the labor force. To ascertain the number of people who would be employed under normal full-employment conditions, therefore, we must be careful to use an estimate of the labor force that allows for the people drawn into the job market by full employment.

Given the "full-employment" number of people with jobs, and the average workweek, we obtain the number of full-employment man-hours. We need only multiply these man-hours by the average output per man-hour to determine the potential GNP.

Output per man-hour, often called "productivity," has grown at about 3 per cent per year in the postwar period. The actual year-by-year changes in productivity are very uneven, because they are composed of two separate elements. On the one hand, they reflect the long-run, smooth productivity trend brought about by a better-educated labor force, advancing technology, and increasing capital per worker; on the other, they contain sharp short-run swings as output rises and falls during the business cycle, with only incomplete and delayed adjustment of employment. Business does not cut back employment as quickly as it cuts back its output. These short-run swings in productivity can add or subtract as much as 3 or 4 per cent in a year, although most of this will of course be offset later on when conditions return to normal.

In summary, potential GNP is determined by the following equation:

$$\text{Potential GNP} = \left(\begin{array}{c}96\% \text{ of normal} \\ \text{labor force}\end{array}\right) \times \left(\begin{array}{c}\text{normal hours of} \\ \text{work per year}\end{array}\right) \times \left(\begin{array}{c}\text{normal} \\ \text{productivity}\end{array}\right)$$

An illustrative calculation for the year 1960 is shown in Table 6–1. Actual employment in 1960 was 69.2 million persons, compared to the 70.8 million who would have been employed under full-employment conditions. They would have worked a bit more than 40 hours a week on the average. Furthermore, output per man-hour would have been slightly higher in 1960 had full-employment conditions prevailed. By multiplying the full-employment work force by normal average yearly hours of work, we get the total man-hours of work that would be

Table 6–1   CALCULATION OF POTENTIAL GNP
IN THE RECESSION YEAR 1960

| Item | Actual | Normal Full-Employment Level | Unit of Measurement | Comment |
|------|--------|------------------------------|---------------------|---------|
| **Labor Input** | | | | |
| 1. Labor force | 73.1 | 73.7 | Millions of persons | 600,000 potential workers were discouraged from entering the labor force by the lack of job opportunities. |
| 2. Employment | 69.2 | 70.8 | Millions of persons | Full employment assumes 96% of labor force employed. Actual 1960 employment was 94.7% of the labor force—unemployment was 5.3%. |
| 3. Weekly hours of work | 39.2 | 40.4 | Hours per week | Actual average hours in 1960 were less than normal because an abnormal number of workers involuntarily worked less than the full workweek. |
| 4. Total man-hours (Line 2 × Line 3 × 52 weeks) | 143.2 | 145.7 | Billions of man-hours | |
| **Productivity** | | | | |
| 5. GNP per man-hour | 3.52 | 3.66 | Dollars per hour | Productivity is higher when full employment is attained; the extra $0.14 allows for this short-run loss in productivity. |
| **Actual and Potential GNP** | | | | |
| 6. Line 4 × Line 5 | 504 | 544 | Billions of dollars | |
| **Gap between Actual and Potential GNP** | | | | |
| | 40 | | Billions of dollars | |

forthcoming in a fully employed economy. The product of potential man-hours worked and normal GNP per man-hour is potential GNP. As the calculations show, 1960 was not a year of full employment; actual GNP fell short of potential GNP by some $40 billion, or more than 7 per cent.

In view of the approximate nature of these calculations, we would probably be safer in not pinning down the potential GNP to such a precise number. We should allow for a 10 per cent error on either side in our calculation of the gap between actual and potential GNP, so that actual GNP fell short of potential by $36 to $44 billion. An increase in aggregate demand could have raised GNP by $36–44 billion. But to score further gains, a rise in potential GNP was necessary.

## THE SOURCES OF GROWTH

### Output, Employment, and Productivity

We have seen that the level of potential GNP depends on two factors: the number of man-hours of labor worked and the productivity of that labor. Let us first examine the long-run determinants of the labor force. We then turn to the factors that influence the rate of economic growth through their impact on labor productivity.

### Labor Input

A nation with a rapidly growing population will also tend, in the long run, to have a rapidly growing labor supply. But the connection between the growth in population and the growth in the amount of labor devoted to economic production is not a simple one.

The amount of labor input depends on three factors: (1) the number of people of working age; (2) the percentage of people of working age who choose to enlist in the labor force, called the *participation rate*; and (3) the number of hours worked per year. All three factors change over time.

Notice, in Fig. 6–1, the exceptionally high participation during World War II, the rather level rate since then, and the continued steady rate that the Department of Labor projects to 1975. The labor force grew rather slowly from 1946 to 1963, only about 800,000 persons a year, but will grow more rapidly from 1964 to 1975, at about 1,400,000 a year. The "baby boom" of the 1940s showed up as a rapid increase in the labor force of the 1960s. As a matter of fact, the relatively slow population growth of the 1920s and the even slower growth during the depression of the 1930s, followed by a rapid growth of population in the 1940s and 1950s, gave us a rather lopsided growth in the labor force during the 1960s. The core of experienced male workers in the 25–55 age bracket grew at a very slow pace, about 0.5 per cent per year, whereas the number of younger

133

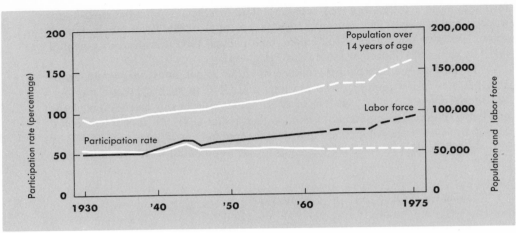

FIG. 6–1 Increase in the working-age population since 1930, their participation rate, and the resultant labor force

people in the labor force is increasing at an annual rate of more than 3.5 per cent. In the second half of the 1960s the economy was struggling to absorb an extraordinary number of inexperienced workers, whereas the prime working-age brackets are rather thin.

The steady participation rate for the working-age population hides some important offsetting trends. Table 6–2 shows the participation rates by age and sex for 1960 and 1968 and the projections for 1975 and 1985.

Participation rates for the younger groups have fallen, because their members stay in school longer. There has also been some decline in the labor force participation rate of people over 65; with society more prosperous, the retirement age for social security lowered from 65 to 62, and with private retirement plans of various kinds widespread, more people can afford to retire before they are forced to do so by ill health. Working in the opposite direction, there has been a very sharp increase in the participation rate among women. In 1940, 28 per cent of women between the ages of 25 and 65 were in the labor force; by 1964 the figure had risen to 43 per cent.

We must also take account of the number of hours worked per year. During most of his existence man has worked a dawn-to-dusk schedule, at least six days a week. In the last century or so, however, this schedule has been sharply curtailed. In 1960 the average member of the labor force worked about 2,000 hours per year—less than 40 hours per week, counting vacations. In 1910 the average work year amounted to 2,700 hours—almost 55 hours per week. Both a shorter work week and the increase in the prevalence and length of vacations have contributed to this reduction. As a consequence, the growth in total man-hours

Table 6–2  LABOR FORCE PARTICIPATION RATES, BY AGE AND SEX,
1960, 1968, AND PROJECTIONS TO 1975 AND 1985

(in per cent)

| Age and Sex | Actual | | Projected | |
|---|---|---|---|---|
| | 1960 | 1968 | 1975 | 1985 |
| Population 16 years and over | 59.2% | 59.8% | 60.1% | 60.8% |
| *Men* | | | | |
| 16 years and over | 82.4 | 79.7 | 79.1 | 79.6 |
| 16–19 years | 58.6 | 57.5 | 56.8 | 56.4 |
| 20–24 years | 88.9 | 85.1 | 83.4 | 82.5 |
| 25–34 years | 96.4 | 95.5 | 96.0 | 96.0 |
| 35–44 years | 96.4 | 96.0 | 96.1 | 96.1 |
| 45–54 years | 94.3 | 93.6 | 94.0 | 94.0 |
| 55–64 years | 85.2 | 82.8 | 81.1 | 79.9 |
| 65 years and over | 32.2 | 26.3 | 23.1 | 21.1 |
| *Women* | | | | |
| 16 years and over | 37.1 | 41.1 | 42.5 | 43.2 |
| 16–19 years | 39.1 | 41.7 | 41.2 | 41.0 |
| 20–24 years | 46.1 | 54.4 | 56.9 | 57.7 |
| 25–34 years | 35.8 | 42.4 | 44.4 | 46.5 |
| 35–44 years | 43.1 | 48.7 | 51.0 | 53.3 |
| 45–54 years | 49.3 | 51.9 | 53.9 | 55.2 |
| 55–64 years | 36.7 | 41.9 | 44.3 | 45.0 |
| 65 years and over | 10.5 | 9.1 | 8.8 | 8.5 |

Source: U.S. Department of Labor.

worked has been much less than the growth in employment. Between 1910 and 1960, for example, employment in the United States approximately doubled, but the total number of hours worked rose by only 50 per cent. We have, as a nation, chosen to take part of the fruits of our rising productivity in the form of greater leisure rather than in physical output.

### The Growth of Productivity

In the long run, rising living standards flow from an increase in output per worker. If output grows only as fast as labor input (i.e., if labor productivity stays unchanged), real income per worker is doomed to remain constant. Output per man-hour in the United States has grown steadily with few interruptions over the period for which we have records. By 1969, output per man-hour was more than five times its level in 1889. Moreover, there is some evidence, as yet inconclusive, that the rate of productivity growth may have accelerated. In each of the periods shown in Table 6–3, for example, productivity rose more rapidly than in the preceding period. Between 1947 and 1969, output per man-hour grew at an average annual rate of 3.2 per cent compared to only 1.7 per cent in the

135

## Table 6–3   THE GROWTH IN OUTPUT PER MAN-HOUR

(Percentage Change per Year)

|  | Entire Period (1889–1969) | 1889 to 1919 | 1919 to 1947 | 1947 to 1969 |
|---|---|---|---|---|
| Output per man-hour (labor productivity) | 2.2 | 1.7 | 2.2 | 3.2 |

period before World War I and the 2.2 per cent growth rate from 1919 to 1947. Twenty years, however, is still too short a period on which to base any firm conclusions about a permanent acceleration in productivity. For the moment, we had best regard this as an intriguing possibility rather than as a demonstrated fact.

### The Causes of Productivity Growth

Pamphleteers and Fourth of July orators to the contrary, there is no simple explanation for the phenomenon of economic growth. The causes of the dramatic rise in output per worker that has characterized the modern history of most industrial nations are many and complex. Advances in scientific and technical knowledge, the spread of education, a steady growth in the stock of physical capital per worker, an expansion of markets which fosters specialization—all these factors contribute. But all are so interrelated that it is exceedingly difficult to isolate the relative importance of each in order to estimate what each has contributed to the over-all result. We can, nevertheless, gain important insights into the growth process by looking at how each of these, and other factors, affect productivity.

A useful way to analyze the phenomenon of rising productivity is to view it in terms of the *production function*. At any point in time, we may think of the economy as possessing a labor force with given education and skills, a stock of productive capital incorporating a particular level of technological advancement, and a specific set of institutional economic arrangements (e.g., small manufacturing establishments and retail outlets versus giant industrial firms or supermarkets). Even without any new technological advances, increases in educational attainments, or changes in organizational arrangements, output per man-hour can be increased by providing the work force with more productive capital. Establishments that are behind the "best" practice in industry can be brought up to date, new rail lines or highways can be built, and so forth. We can think of a *production function* for the nation as a whole, which relates output per man-hour to the amount of productive capital per worker. A series of such production functions is illustrated in Fig. 6–2. As the amount of capital available to each worker is increased, output per man-hour rises from point $A$ on production function 1 through the points labeled $X$, $Y$, and $Z$.

The continued addition of *more* capital of the same kind, however, with no

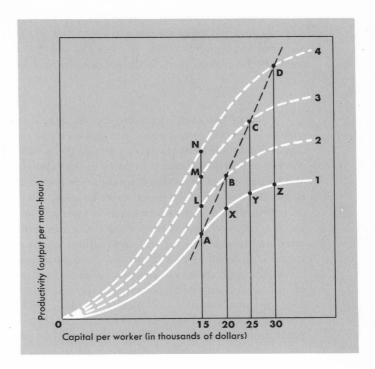

**FIG. 6–2** Shifts in production functions

change in technology or in the capabilities of the labor force, would soon bring diminishing returns. Each additional increment of capital would yield progressively smaller increments in productivity. To say this another way, a simple increase in the *quantity* of capital, with no change in its *quality* or in the quality of the labor force, would yield increases in productivity, but in ever-diminishing increments. The production function, in other words, "tops out."

Historically, of course, technology has not remained constant. New scientific and technical knowledge has made it possible to produce better products and to use resources more effectively. The growth of education has upgraded the quality of the labor force, and changes in the organization and market structure of industry have improved the efficiency of the economic system. As a consequence, new production functions have continually superseded the old ones. In Fig. 6–2 this phenomenon is shown by the rise in the production functions from 1 to 4. As the production function rises, the same quantity of capital per worker yields higher productivity, because the *quality* of both the capital and the labor force has been improved. In this case, output per man-hour would trace the path *A, L, M, N* in Fig. 6–2.

*The process of economic development in the United States has been characterized both by shifts in the production function and by substantial increases*

137

*in the quantity of capital available per worker.* As a consequence, productivity has traced a path like that of the line *A, B, C, D.* Let us examine, in turn, the increase in capital available per worker and the various factors that have made possible the upward shifts in the production function.

One of the chief characteristics of industrial growth has been a sharp increase in the stock of capital per worker. The medieval artisan had, at best, a few rudimentary tools. In most parts of the world today the major investment of the typical farmer is still a mule or an ox. But the modern industrial worker in the United States has at his disposal an immense capital in machinery and equipment, not only directly in the tools he uses, but indirectly in the electric power he is furnished and the transportation system that delivers his finished product to the market. The same is true of the American farmer, or at least of those farmers who supply the bulk of our agricultural needs. The average value of capital invested in large Midwestern cash grain farms, for example, is over $100,000.

Rising productivity involves an increase in our ability to harness the forces of nature, for supplying power, transporting goods, and manipulating materials. This, in turn, requires not merely scientific and technical knowledge, but the provision of expensive plant and equipment. It requires, in other words, capital.[2] And capital goods are not "free." They must be produced, using labor, materials, and machines that might otherwise have been utilized to turn out consumer goods. Providing the labor force with an increasing supply of machinery and equipment involves *saving*—the nation must refrain from consuming part of its output so that resources may be free to produce capital goods.

In an economy with growing productivity there are three types of requirements for capital goods, and therefore for saving. First, capital must be provided simply to replace that part of the existing plant and equipment which is used up each year in the production process. Second, as the labor force grows, new plant and equipment must be provided each year to keep the stock of capital per worker intact; if the labor force grows at 2 per cent per year, then the stock of capital must grow at the same rate if the amount of capital per worker is not to deteriorate. These first two capital requirements are needed simply to maintain the status quo. In the United States, however, the capital stock has risen *faster* than the labor force; capital per worker has increased fairly steadily, between 1 and 2 per cent per year during most of the period since the Civil War. This rise in capital per worker is one of the important reasons for the growth in productivity. There is, therefore, a third capital requirement—namely, an amount of investment sufficient to increase the stock of capital per worker.

---

[2] In the discussion that follows it will be important to remember that we use the term *capital* to represent the total *stock* of machinery, equipment, plant, and other productive goods on hand. The term *investment* represents the annual *flow* of newly produced capital goods that replace part of the existing capital stock or add to that stock.

An example may help make clear how these three capital requirements relate to total investment and saving. Let us assume an economy with the following characteristics.

1. GNP                      =    $ 500  billion
2. Capital stock            =    $ 750  billion
3. Labor force              =        50  million workers
4. Capital stock per worker
   (2 ÷ 3)                  =    $  15  thousand
5. Labor force growth       =    2% per year (1 million new workers)
6. 4% of the capital stock wears out each year.

Under these assumptions, we get the following capital requirements:

1. Replacement (4% of $750 billion)                                     =    $30  billion
2. Capital required to provide the new workers with plant
   and equipment (1 million new workers × $15,000)                      =    15  billion
3. If capital stock per worker is to increase so that pro-
   ductivity may rise, additional capital is needed. Let us
   assume a 1.5% per year rise in capital stock per
   worker. This implies an extra $225 of capital stock per
   worker, or 1.5 of $15,000 × 51 million workers                       =    11  billion
                                                                               ——
   Total investment                                                          $56 billion
   Total investment as percentage of GNP                                     11%

In the economy described above, 11 per cent of total GNP is devoted to gross investment in order to provide for capital replacement, and an increase in capital stock per worker. In turn, 11 per cent of GNP has to be saved—i.e., *not* consumed—so that resources will be available to produce the investment goods. That part of investment devoted to furnishing the new entrants to the labor force with the same average capital as already exists is called "capital-widening" ($15 billion in our example).[3] Investment which increases the capital–labor ratio is called capital-deepening ($11 billion in our example).

### Investment and Economic Growth in the United States

Professor Kuznets has published a monumental study of capital formation in the United States. In Table 6–4, some of the major relationships that he has found between capital, labor force, and productivity are summarized.

[3] This simple example illustrates one of the problems posed for poor countries by rapid population growth. In order simply to maintain living standards, output per worker must be prevented from falling. This, in turn, requires that the capital stock per worker must be kept constant. If the labor force is growing very rapidly, this condition requires the nation to invest a substantial sum in new plant and equipment each year simply to hold its own with respect to per-capita living standards. In a poor country, the saving rate is likely to be quite low—it is hard to save much when you are poor. But with rapid population growth, much of those scarce savings must be used to keep capital per worker from declining and little is left over to raise capital stock per worker, output per man-hour, and living standards.

Since the Civil War, the *gross* capital stock (capital stock *before* allowance for depreciation) has risen much more rapidly than the labor force; in the decade after World War II capital per worker was *four* times larger than in the decade following the Civil War. The *net* capital stock (after depreciation) also rose, but not so rapidly, attaining a level almost *three* times that of 80 years ago. The growth of capital during the Great Depression of the 1930s was quite a bit lower than during other periods—indeed, on a net basis, capital per worker declined during these years. And in the first decade after World War II, the capital stock, although increasing faster than during the depression, grew at a slower rate than during the decades prior to 1929.

The growth pattern of the capital stock is reflected in the investment data in the last two columns at the top of Table 6–4. During the period before 1929, gross investment—which includes both replacement and net additions to the capital stock—ranged between 22 and 25 per cent of gross national product; net investment accounted for 11 to 15 per cent of net national product. This was sufficient to provide a sharp increase in the capital stock and to raise available capital per worker. In the depression of the 1930s and during World War II, gross investment, as a percentage of GNP, fell sharply, to the point where it was

Table 6–4 CAPITAL STOCK, LABOR FORCE, AND PRODUCTIVITY, 1869–1955

| Period | Capital Stock per Member of the Labor Force (In 1929 dollars) | | Investment as a Percentage of Output | |
|---|---|---|---|---|
| | Gross | Net | Gross | Net |
| 1869 to 1878 | $ 3,800 | $2,300 | 22.9% | 15.1% |
| 1889 to 1898 | 6,000 | 3,200 | 25.1 | 15.2 |
| 1909 to 1918 | 9,100 | 4,900 | 22.1 | 11.9 |
| 1929 to 1939 | 13,000 | 6,100 | 13.4 | 1.9 |
| 1946 to 1955 | 15,300 | 6,000 | 17.3 | 4.8 |

*Growth of Capital, Capital per Worker, and Productivity (Percentage growth per decade)*

| | Gross Capital Stock | Gross Capital Stock per Worker | Labor Productivity (Output per Man-hour) |
|---|---|---|---|
| 1869 to 1889 | 60.8% | 21.7% | n.a. |
| 1889 to 1909 | 59.4 | 23.0 | 22.7% |
| 1909 to 1929 | 42.1 | 24.9 | 17.7 |
| 1929 to 1946 | 20.6 | 8.4 | 24.9 |
| 1946 to 1955 | 36.5 | 19.2 | 42.8 |

Source: All data from Simon Kuznets, *Capital in the American Economy* (Princeton, N.J.: National Bureau of Economic Research, 1961) except for productivity, which is taken from John Kendrick, *Productivity Trends in the United States* (Princeton, N.J.: National Bureau of Economic Research, 1961), and the Bureau of Labor Statistics, *Trends in Output per Man-hour in the Private Economy* (Washington, D.C.: U.S. Dept. of Labor, BLS Bulletin 1249, 1959).

barely sufficient to cover replacement requirements. As a consequence, net investment dropped to almost zero, and since the labor force kept growing, the net capital stock per worker declined. After World War II, the investment share of GNP rose again, but not back to its earlier levels. And, reflecting this, the rate of growth in capital per worker was much lower in the postwar period than in the years before 1929.

One of the most significant features of Table 6–4 is the data on productivity. We pointed out earlier that rising productivity is associated with a rising capital stock per worker. But we also said that the relationship was not very rigid. Notice, in Table 6–4, that rate of growth in productivity during the 1946–1955 period was higher than in the earlier periods, even though the rate of growth in capital per worker was less than in all the periods prior to 1929. Clearly, a number of factors other than the volume of investment in capital goods contribute to rising productivity and economic growth.[4]

### Progress of Science and Technology

We have stressed, so far, the importance of rising capital per worker as a source of the growth in productivity. But it is not merely that workers now have at their disposal *more* capital goods—they have *better* capital goods. The accumulation of capital does not consist chiefly in providing the labor force with more of the same kind of machinery and equipment. Rather, it involves the acquisition of different, and usually more technologically advanced, kinds of capital goods. Growth in productivity, in other words, has involved a shift upward in the production function as well as a movement along the function.

Technological progress takes many forms. It is the development of new methods of producing given products, through the use of more efficient machinery, more effective organization of the process, and greater specialization of labor, made possible by expansion of markets. Equally important, technological progress consists of the development of new products for the consumer and new materials for the producer.

The accumulation of capital and technological progress are closely linked. Imagine, if you will, that the advance of science and technology had been halted in 1910. Productivity could still have been increased. More of the same kind of capital could have been accumulated—greater trackage for steam railroads; additional canals; electric motors (then already in existence) could have replaced some steam power, and so on. Moreover, in 1910, not all factories or plants were

---

[4]Professor Robert A. Gordon has recently pointed out that these data, and other similar data on the capital stock, seriously *understate* the size of the capital stock in the years since World War II, since they leave out of account the large volume of plant and equipment bought for armaments production during the war and turned over at cut-rate prices to private industries for commercial use after the war. Even if we correct for the "error" that Professor Gordon has noted, however, it is still probably correct to say that the growth of capital stock per worker in the postwar decade was somewhat less than in earlier, predepression years.

up to date. At any given moment, "average practice" in industry always lags behind "best practice," so that over-all national productivity could have advanced as the great bulk of firms caught up with the leaders. Nevertheless, the rate of productivity growth would have soon begun to slow down, as existing technology became fully utilized. Without the upward shift in the production function which technological progress makes possible, productivity would, at best, have increased slowly along a path like $A, X, Y, Z$ in Fig. 6–2.

Imagine, now, the opposite situation in 1910—scientific and technological progress continues, but for one reason or another, there is not sufficient saving to permit any increase in capital per worker. In this case it is more difficult to say what would have happened. To some extent the shortage of capital might have provided incentives to develop production techniques that economized on the use of capital. Productivity could have continued to advance. Nevertheless, it is almost certain that the growth of productivity would have been very much slower than what has actually occurred. Many of the major industries that experienced particularly rapid growth after 1910 required especially heavy capital investment per worker—electric utilities, petroleum, chemicals, and trucking (counting public investment in highways) are prime examples.

Thus, although the accumulation of capital and technological progress can be thought of as two distinct sources of economic growth, they are intimately related. Without the other, each could make only a limited contribution to growth. Much of technological progress is embodied in new capital. Much of the contribution of new investment to economic growth is due not to the additional capital per se, but to the new technology that it carries with it and that could not be introduced without it.

In the last section we pointed out the apparent paradox that in the postwar years the rate of productivity growth did not decline even though the rate of growth in capital per worker was substantially lower than in earlier periods. One reason for this may be that technological progress has speeded up. Some economists also believe that the nature of technological progress has changed. In the earlier phases of economic growth, most new techniques required massive additions to the stock of capital. Compare the capital investment in railroads with that involved in stage coaches, for example. These economists feel that the nature of most modern technical changes is such, however, that similar massive injections of capital are no longer required. The new technique of oxygenation in the steel industry, for example, tends to reduce capital requirements. Such techniques are capital-saving as well as labor-saving. This is one possible explanation for the continuation—and perhaps even acceleration—of the rate of productivity growth in the face of a slower rise in the capital–labor ratio. So far, however, the techniques of economic and statistical analysis have not been able to prove or disprove the contention that most new techniques are capital-saving in nature. It must remain, for the moment, an interesting hypothesis.

One modern development does suggest that the pace of technical progress may have speeded up. In 1940 identifiable expenditures on research and development by business, government, and universities were about $1 billion. In 1969 they exceeded $25 billion. Not all this rise in expenditures represents an increase in the kind of research and development that will result in new commercial or industrial techniques. In earlier years more of the research was undertaken as part of the production process by individuals outside of business firms. Part of this increase, therefore, simply reflects a more formal organization of research and development. Also, a considerable part of the rise in research and development expenditures has been devoted to military and space objectives and, although there are civilian uses, the contribution of the bulk of this type of research to economic growth is questionable. Even after all these qualifications, however, it is hard to believe that this massive increase in research expenditures will not have some effect on the rate of technical progress.

### Education and Labor Force Skills

As we have seen, economic growth requires a steady advance in the amount and complexity of the capital used in the production and distribution process. The achievement of a sustained upward shift in the production function requires that advancing technology be accompanied by an increase in the education and skills of the labor force. The modern American economy could not be operated by the labor force of 50 years ago—its skills and training would not have been sufficient. This is mirrored in the experience of those American business firms that establish plants in less-developed countries. These plants are modern and up to date, yet their productivity is usually much lower than the same plants operating in the United States.

The growth in the quality of the labor force necessary for economic growth does not merely relate to particular specialized skills. Today's American economy requires a much higher proportion of high school and college graduates than the economy of 1900, or even 1930. Today more than two out of every three young persons entering the labor force have at least completed high school. Fifty years ago only one out of five had done so. Whereas only 5 per cent of young people of working age currently fail to complete elementary school, 40 per cent failed to do so a half-century ago. Not only has there been a steady increase in the number of school years completed, but the number of days of school per year has increased. A century ago, school attendance came second, after the necessary chores on the farm, in the family store, or even in the factory, were completed.

If we take into account the increase both in the number of school years and the number of school days per year, it turns out that the average member of the 1960 labor force had spent 2½ times as many days in school as had his predecessor 50 years earlier. Although we do not have data going back to the nineteenth century, it is clear that the 1910 labor force was itself better educated than the labor force in 1860. It is not at all unlikely that the 1960 labor force had some four to five times the education of its 1860 counterpart.

143

There is a direct relation between education and income. In 1961 the average income of a man with a high school education was 47 per cent greater than one who had finished only the eighth grade (Fig. 6–3). The average college graduate earned 30 per cent more than the high school graduate and post-college education yielded still higher incomes. These differences in average earnings roughly reflect differences in productivity, and therefore, to the extent that the higher income is due to education, it can be said that education raises productivity.

Not all the differences in productivity, represented by the income differences in Fig. 6–3, can be attributed to education alone. Differences in number of school years completed probably reflect, to some extent, differences in native ability. College graduates tend to have a higher I.Q. than high school graduates, whose I.Q. in turn is higher than those who finish only elementary school. Moreover, college graduates are more likely to come from families with higher incomes—their initial opportunities are greater, on the average, than those from lower-income families. Nevertheless, after all these qualifications, there is little doubt that additional schooling increases earnings and productivity. Professor Gary Becker of Columbia University, for example, has calculated that the monetary return from a college education, in terms of higher earnings, is about equal to the average rate of return on business investments.[5] And this calculation includes

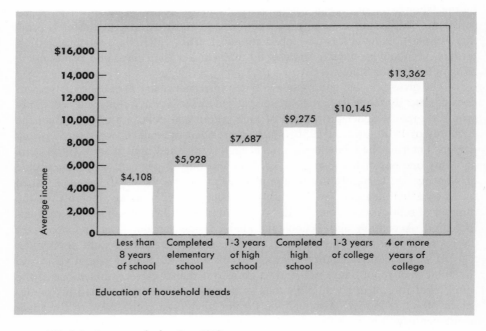

**FIG. 6–3** Income and education, 1969

[5]Gary S. Becker, *Human Capital*, Columbia University Press, New York, 1964.

as the cost of education not only the direct costs of tuition, books, and extra room and board, but also the earnings forgone during attendance at college.

When we take into account such evidence as we have on the additional income resulting from an added year of schooling—and remember that most of this represents added productivity—then it is clear that the sharp increase in the educational attainments of the labor force over the past century has made a major contribution to economic growth. This emphasis is not meant to imply that economic growth is the sole, or even the primary, value of education. A civilized society—even one with primitive production methods—places a high value on education for its own sake. Witness, for example, the ancient Greeks. In a sense, the growth contribution of education is a bonus. It is an added benefit we derive from doing something we believe to be desirable in its own right.

**Measuring the Contribution of**

**Various Factors to Economic Growth**

In recent years economists have for the first time attempted to measure quantitatively the importance of some of the major factors that contribute to economic growth. Professors Robert Solow of M.I.T. and John Kendrick of George Washington University, and Edward Denison at the Brookings Institution, have been the pioneers in this work.

Each of the studies measuring contributions to growth starts with the crucial assumption that the income of a particular factor of production measures its contribution to output. Thus the rate of return on capital is taken as a measure of capital's contribution to output, and the differences in income among people with differing amounts of education are used as a basis for measuring the contribution of education.

Edward Denison's study is the most comprehensive to date. Table 6–5 summarizes his results. The 2.3 per cent growth in output per man-hour between 1929 and 1957 is allocated among the major contributors to that growth. Notice that Denison gives a good bit of weight to the importance of lower hours of work as a factor that has increased the productivity of the labor force. Denison's "advance in knowledge" (the last item in the table) is the same as our "scientific and technological progress."

**Table 6–5** SOURCES OF GROWTH IN OUTPUT

PER MAN-HOUR, 1929–1957

| | Contribution to Growth | Percentage of Total |
|---|---|---|
| Average annual growth in output per man-hour | 2.3% | 100% |
| Increase in capital per worker | .3 | 13 |
| Increase in education | .7 | 30 |
| Effect of lower hours of work | .3 | 13 |
| Advance in knowledge, expansion of markets, and all other factors | 1.0 | 44 |

145

The most striking fact about Denison's study is the importance it assigns to education. In making his calculations Denison assumed that 60 per cent of the difference in incomes among people with different years of schooling is due to education, and the remainder to associated differences in native ability, family background, and the like. A lower assumption would reduce his estimate of the importance of education, and conversely, a higher assumption would raise it.

Denison also attributes a surprisingly small growth contribution to the increase in capital per worker. This result is due to two factors. First, over this particular period, the increase in the amount of capital per worker was relatively small, as we saw in Table 6–4. Second, Denison makes no allowance for the joint effects of capital and technology. He treats them as separate elements, attributing none of the technological progress to the extra capital, even though, in fact, some of it must be embodied in capital to come into use.

None of the recent studies attempting to allocate to various causal factors the responsibility for economic growth can provide us with precise answers. They incorporate a number of assumptions that are difficult if not impossible to check. And some of the data leave much to be desired. Nevertheless, they are a promising beginning for further research directed toward narrowing the range of arbitrary assumptions and furnishing more accurate data. And, even at this stage, such studies provide some long-needed quantitative information about the possible effects of various policies directed toward increasing the rate of growth.

## POLICIES TO INCREASE
## THE RATE OF GROWTH

Between 1947 and 1969 the rate of growth in GNP (in constant dollars) was 4 per cent per year. Assuming full employment, it is probable that without any major change in economic policies the economy could grow at perhaps 4.25 per cent per year during the first half of the 1970s. Given the increase in the growth of the labor force that began in 1965, and a continuation of the modest downward trend in average hours worked, we can expect total man-hours worked to rise at slightly more than 1.5 per cent per year. If postwar experience is any guide to future productivity gains forthcoming under full-employment conditions, we might expect a rise in productivity of about 2.8 per cent per year. The assumed growth in man-hours and in productivity together would yield an annual GNP growth rate of 4.25 per cent.

Let us now assume that it would be desirable to increase that rate of growth. Taking the growth in man-hours worked as given, any increase in the growth rate would require a rise in productivity larger than the projected 2.8 per cent per year. What policies might accomplish that goal?

**Increasing Investment**

The first and most obvious requirement is an increase in the rate of growth of capital per worker. This in turn requires an increase in the proportion of GNP devoted to productive investment, by business and by government. One of the conclusions flowing from all the studies cited above is that it takes a large increase in investment to accomplish a fairly small increase in the growth rate. Denison has calculated, for example, that an increase in net investment of about $7 billion (which raises the share of GNP going to net investment by one-fourth—from about 4 per cent to about 5 per cent) would add 0.1 per cent to the growth rate. Since a rise in investment also speeds up the rate at which new technology is incorporated into the production process, this estimate may be on the low side. Even if we double it—getting an increase of 0.2 instead or 0.1—this still appears to be a slight result. But think of it this way. An additional 0.2 added to the growth rate is really a 5 per cent increase in growth (0.2/4.0). Moreover, the magic of compound interest raises the importance of that "little" 0.2 per cent as the years go by. Twenty-five years from now GNP would be $100 billion higher with a 4.2 per cent growth rate than it would be with a 4 per cent growth rate. Although we cannot effect very large changes in the growth rate by modest changes in investment, what appear to be small increases in the growth rate are quite important for the magnitude of future GNP.

Assuming that we wished to raise the proportion of GNP devoted to investment, what could the government do? Basically, two kinds of policies can be used, fiscal or monetary. First, additional incentives and an increased supply of funds must be provided to stimulate and finance business investment. With a reduction in taxes on corporate profits, some investments that were not quite profitable enough to be undertaken at the higher tax rates would now be profitable. Take a firm, for example, with a number of investment opportunities which are estimated to yield the following profit returns:

| List of Possible Investment Projects | | Expected Rate of Return | |
|---|---|---|---|
| *Cost of New Plant or Equipment Involved (Thousands of dollars)* | | *Before Taxes* | *After Taxes (with 50% Corporate Profits Tax)* |
| (1) | 200 | 34% | 17% |
| (2) | 100 | 28 | 14 |
| (3) | 150 | 22 | 11 |
| (4) | 300 | 18 | 9 |
| (5) | 60 | 16 | 8 |
| (6) | 100 | 12 | 6 |

Let us assume that the firm will make only investments that yield a return of 10 per cent or more *after taxes*. With the corporate tax rate at 50 per cent, investment projects 1 through 3 pass this test, but the others do not. If, however, the corporate profits tax were lowered from 50 to 33 per cent, then projects 4 and 5 would yield more than a 10 per cent return after tax, and would under our assumptions be undertaken (their after-tax yields would rise to 12 and 10.7 per cent, respectively). Moreover, the reduction in corporate profits taxes would leave corporations with more funds to finance the added investment.

However, we are assuming that the economy is already at full employment. Under these conditions, an increase in the demand for investment goods, with everything else constant, would lead to inflation, since total demand would exceed the economy's capacity to produce. Or put this another way. If all resources are currently being used, then an increase in the amount of resources devoted to investment must be offset by a decrease in resources devoted to consumption or government spending. Thus a policy of reducing taxes on corporations in order to stimulate investment would have to be accompanied either by an increase in taxes on consumers (in order to lower consumption) or a decrease in government spending. (And since we are interested in promoting growth, we would not wish to reduce the government outlays that are themselves of an investment character, such as roads and schools; we should have to pick other government outlays as candidates for reduction. A balanced growth program requires an expansion of both private and public investment.)

Growth is not free. If we wish to devote a larger proportion of our resources to producing growth-promoting investment goods, we must be satisfied with a smaller proportion going to consumption or government services (always assuming, of course, that the economy is already at full employment). The fiscal policy requirements of growth are simply a reflection of this. When we reduce business taxes to stimulate growth, we must also raise taxes on consumers or curtail government outlays on current services.

Another combination of government policies designed to produce a faster rate of growth in investment involves the use of an easy-money, low-interest-rate policy together with a tight budgetary policy. Low interest rates and easy availability of credit tend to stimulate investment. But assuming again that we start with full employment, it would be necessary to plan for a tighter budget, with a larger surplus (or smaller deficit) than would otherwise have been the case in order to offset the inflationary impact of the increase in investment spending. Investment is encouraged by easy-money policies, and consumption or government spending is restrained by a tight budget policy.

### Improving Education

Education is another area in which public policy can influence the rate of growth. As we mentioned earlier, current economic growth stems in part from the increase in years of schooling. Mere maintenance of the historical rate of growth requires a continuing increase in the educational attainment of the labor force. Speeding up the contribution of education to economic growth would require an *acceleration* in the increase of educational attainment. Beyond a point, the increase in the "quantity" of education, through more years in school, will reach a limit. There are still large segments of the population, of course, who leave school before they have exhausted their capacity for education. The school dropout problem has its economic as well as its social disadvantages. Nevertheless, as time goes on, the contribution of education to economic growth will have to be more and more an increase in quality rather than in quantity.

Stepping up the growth contribution of education would not be costless. Additional facilities and more and better qualified teachers are not to be had merely by wishing. Furthermore, from the viewpoint of growth, education has a very slow pay-off. The average male spends more than 40 years in the labor force. Suppose, for example, that we started now to take action that added one new year of schooling, on the average, for those persons currently entering the labor force. Ten years from now little more than a fourth of the labor force would have yet benefited from this new policy, and the economic loss (from the reduction in the labor force attributable to the fact that people stayed in school longer) would still be more than the economic gain. By 1990, half the labor force would have been affected by the new policy, and the gain in greater productivity would be exceeding the loss in the number of available workers. Only by the year 2025 would the entire labor force benefit from the new policy. Denison, in his tough-minded manner, has calculated that such a policy would, by the year 2025, have added perhaps 0.1 per cent to the growth rate.

The foregoing is not meant to disparage the desirability of devoting additional resources to education. In many things we must take the long view. Our own standards of living, after all, derive in part from the resources our parents and grandparents devoted to improving the educational system. Expenditures devoted to education are no less an investment in future growth than the building of a new factory or a new dam. If the entire society is to share in the fruits of growth, all workers must be equipped to use these new technological advances. And, as we noted above, a 0.1 per cent addition to the growth rate is no mean achievement. Nevertheless, it is important to bear in mind that economic growth has costs in terms of present resources. Accelerating the rate of growth is not an easy matter; we should be aware of its costs as well as its benefits if we are to make rational decisions about what policies the nation ought to pursue in the area of economic growth.

### Other Policies Affecting Growth

Policies directed at investment and education do not exhaust the list of things that can be done by the government and the private economy to promote accelerated economic growth.

In the first place, to repeat a crucial point once more, a sharp increase in economic potential that is not accompanied by an equal increase in the demand for goods and services will simply lead to higher unemployment and excess capacity. In turn, a slack economy dulls the incentives for further growth. When plants are idle for want of market demand, businesses will quite properly become cautious about adding additional capacity. High rates of unemployment lead—again quite naturally—to hostility toward automation, creating a climate in which job protection, featherbedding, and rigid work rules slow down the advance in productivity. Policies directed toward a faster growth in economic potential will be self-defeating unless they are accompanied by a policy that allows demand to expand at an equally rapid pace.

Another area in which government policies can play a major part, either to promote or to hinder economic growth, relates to the mobility of resources. The essence of growth is change. Anything that tends to freeze workers and capital in existing industries or localities is bound in the long run to hinder economic growth. Farm policies that encourage excess farm production year in and year out and tie up agricultural resources that ought to be employed elsewhere not only slow down economic growth, but in the long run hurt the very farmers they are designed to help. Tariff policies that continue decade after decade to shelter inefficient industries and to keep labor and capital tied up in relatively unproductive occupations are another obstacle. Equally bad for economic growth are many governmental policies that regulate minimum transportation rates to prevent effective competition among railroads, trucks, and barge lines and, in all too many cases, guarantee traffic to the least efficient means of transportation.

This is not to say that individual firms and workers may not need some protection against the rude winds of economic change. There is no economic or political principle stating that economic growth must necessarily take precedence over all other considerations. The creation of new and more efficient industries and techniques at the expense of old ones benefits society as a whole. But it harshly penalizes those whose jobs are destroyed or whose savings are frozen in obsolete capital. Society, which reaps the benefits of this change, owes some protection to those at whose expense progress occurs. Unemployment compensation, worker retraining programs, and government assistance to "distressed" areas can alleviate the pains of economic growth. As a general rule, both economic growth and social justice are far better served by policies that make it easier for workers and businessmen to adjust to change than by "protectionist" policies whose aim is to prevent change.

To a very large extent, the rate of economic growth is determined by saving and investment decisions, inventive talent, and willingness to take risks on the part of millions of individuals and business firms. Government policy can influence the results of all these individual actions. But it cannot create out of thin air the attitudes and habits that growth requires. This is why there is no pat formula for growth and why so many of the problems of economic development are not purely economic problems.

## GROWTH AND BUSINESS CYCLES

In Chapters 3 and 4, we stressed that actual output would tend to equal potential output if all the income generated in the production of potential output were spent on either consumption or investment goods (leaving aside the government for simplicity's sake). Put another way, that part of potential GNI *not* spent on consumption goods *must* be spent on investment goods if total spending is to be high enough to purchase total potential output. Therefore, an economy that saves part of its income must spend an equal amount on new capital goods if unemployment and recession are to be avoided. But in this chapter we have seen that investment adds to economic potential; investment this year, by increasing productivity and industrial capacity, leads to a higher potential output next year. Next year, therefore, to avoid excess capacity and unemployment, spending must be higher than it was this year. But this means still greater investment spending, and still higher capacity the third year, and so on each year.

This process is shown in Fig. 6–4. Let us assume a certain potential GNP (= GNI) in year 1. Some portion of the income generated in the production of the GNP is saved—i.e., not spent on consumption goods. If aggregate demand is to be high enough to purchase the output of the economy, then investment in new plant, equipment, housing, and the like, must equal the amount saved. But this new capital adds to the nation's capacity to produce; in year 2 economic potential is greater than in year 1. Saving out of this potential GNI will also be higher, and so investment must rise in year 2 if aggregate demand is to equal the new potential. This in turn raises potential GNP in the third year, and so the process continues. If at any time investment or consumption spending fail to increase, then actual GNP will be below potential, excess capacity will appear, the incentive to invest will be reduced, and investment may decline. If this occurs, GNP will de-

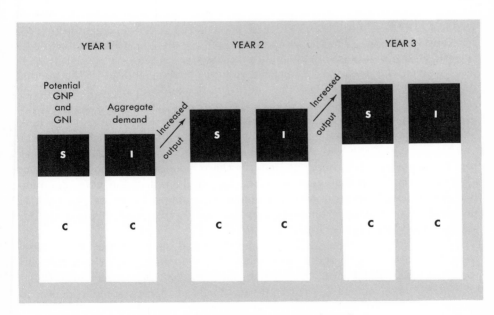

FIG. 6–4   Economic growth and the problem of aggregate demand

cline by an amount determined by the size of the multiplier. The moral of this story is simple. An economy that saves part of its income must, in the long run, either grow or decline. It cannot stand still for long. The requirement for economic stability is not merely that we have a *high* level of investment, but that we have a continuously *rising* level to absorb the rising level of saving. And in view of the volatility of investment expenditures, this requirement is not easy to fulfill. It is here that we come full circle to the point stressed in Chapter 1—the very features of our economy that lead to economic growth also make it vulnerable to economic instability.

The fact that the very saving–investment process that is crucial to economic growth also complicates the problem of economic stability does not necessarily mean that major recessions must be the inevitable accompaniment of growth. Chapter 4 pointed out the numerous stabilizing factors now built into the United States economy. Even more important, we saw that intelligent fiscal and monetary policy on the part of the government can contain and offset within fairly narrow limits economic forces that if unchecked would lead to depression. We are no longer faced with the choice between growth on the one hand and stability on the other. We can have both. If we do not, the fault lies with us, not with economic forces beyond our ken or control.

## SUMMARY

When the economy is operating below its potential, an increase in aggregate demand will raise output. But for long-run economic growth to occur, potential GNP must rise. The rate at which potential GNP grows depends upon the rate of growth of labor input and of productivity.

Three basic factors determine the volume of labor input: (1) the number of people of working age; (2) the rate of participation of those people in the labor force; and (3) average working hours. Participation rates of particular groups do change, but the over-all participation rate does not seem to have altered sharply in the past half-century. The change in working-age population has been, and probably will continue to be, the dominant factor affecting the labor force. The postwar baby boom has led to a sharp increase in the labor force since 1965, to about 1.4 million persons a year. During the past half-century the number of hours worked per year has declined from almost 55 hours per week to less than 40 at the present time. Working hours will probably continue to decline slowly, chiefly as a result of longer vacations.

In the long run, rising living standards depend upon the growth of output per unit of labor input (productivity of labor). *Productivity* must rise if real per-capita income is to increase. The annual gain in productivity in the United States since 1890 has averaged 2.2 per cent per year, and there is some evidence, as yet inconclusive, for believing the rate of gain has accelerated.

It is useful to think of the determinants of productivity gain in terms of the *production function*. The production function relates the level of productivity in the economy to the amount of capital per worker, given the state of technology and the skills of the labor force. The larger the stock of capital per worker, the higher the level of productivity. With unchanged technology and labor force skills, however, each additional increment of capital per worker would yield progressively smaller increments to productivity. Historically, productivity gains have come from two basic sources: (1) a movement along the production function brought about by increases in capital per worker, and (2) a shift upward in the production function arising from a number of causes, but chiefly from advancing science and technology and from improvements in the educational attainment of the labor force.

In the United States the capital stock has, over the past century, expanded faster than the labor force. In addition to replacing worn-out capital and equipping the new members of a growing labor force with a stock of plant and equipment, investment has been sufficient to yield a substantial increase in capital per worker. The rise in capital per worker was much more rapid prior to World War I than subsequently. Nevertheless, this slowing of the rate of growth in capital per worker has not been accompanied by any retardation in the rate of productivity gain.

Productivity has risen not merely on account of increases in capital per worker (movement *along* a given production). Its rise also stems from advances in science and technology and increases in the skills and educational attainments of the labor force (causing an *upward shift* in the production function). Advancing science and technology have made it possible to equip the labor force not merely with additional capital but with more productive capital. In turn, the labor force has been able to adapt to the sharply increasing complexity of the production process, chiefly because average educational attainments have risen dramatically over the past hundred years. All the evidence we have indicates that education has made a major contribution to the growth in productivity.

Policies can be devised to speed up the rate of economic growth. A faster rise in capital per worker would accelerate the growth in productivity. Tax and monetary policies can be designed to achieve such a goal. But, assuming the economy to be already at full employment, an increase in investment must be accompanied by a decrease in consumption (or in consumption-like government outlays). Thus, tax rate decreases designed to stimulate investment (at full employment) would have to be accompanied by tax rate increases aimed at consumers, or by reductions in government outlays of a noninvestment nature. Similarly, a step-up in education or in research and development expenditures would divert toward these growth-oriented activities resources that could have been used to produce consumer goods. An acceleration of the growth rate, in other words, is not free; it "costs" in terms of resources.

None of the foregoing is meant to suggest that a decision to raise the rate of growth would be undesirable. Even a small increase in the growth rate, when compounded over a number of years, has a substantial impact on GNP. And we should not forget that our own high living standards stem in no small way from the willingness of our fathers and grandfathers to devote part of their limited resources to growth-promoting uses. All we wish to point out is that accelerating the rate of growth is not an easy matter. We must be aware of its costs as well as its benefits, if we are to make intelligent decisions about public policies in this area.

The problem of economic stability is not independent of the problem of economic growth. To avoid unemployment, actual GNP must equal potential GNP. For this to be possible, investment spending must be sufficient to match the saving forthcoming at a full-employment level of income. But investment also adds to economic potential. Consequently, the attainment of full employment in one year carries with it the certainty of a higher potential GNP the next year. An even larger volume of investment will then be needed to make sure that aggregate demand equals the new potential. Thus, a full-employment economy must necessarily be a growing economy.

In an economy where consumption accounted for 100 per cent of income, where there were no saving and no investment, there would be no major problem of economic instability. But, of course, there would also be little growth. To grow, some portion of income must be saved and devoted to increasing the nation's stock of capital. Once habits of saving are built into the economy, economic instability becomes more probable.

The saving–investment process, which is central to economic growth, does indeed raise stability problems. But we have seen how intelligent fiscal policy can, within fairly narrow limits, contain and offset recession forces. We do not have to make the choice between economic growth and economic stability. We can have both.

# Selected Readings

A thorough and detailed explanation of the national income accounts is contained in Richard and Nancy Ruggles, *National Income Accounts and Income Analysis* (New York: McGraw-Hill Book Company, 1956). The United States Department of Commerce publishes summary up-to-date national income data in its quarterly *Survey of Current Business*. Detailed tables on the various components of GNP and GNI from 1929 onward are contained in the Department of Commerce volume, *Income and Output* (Washington, D.C.: Government Printing Office, 1958). Each year the July issue of the *Survey of Current Business* brings the detailed tables up to date. The statistical appendix to the annual *Economic Report of the President* (published each January by the Government Printing Office) also provides a convenient summary of the most important national income accounts data.

The classic work on national income theory is J. M. Keynes, *The General Theory of Employment, Interest and Money* (1936). This is a very difficult book for the beginning student, however. A very useful interpretation of *The General Theory* is provided by Alvin Hansen, *Guide to Keynes* (New York: McGraw-Hill Book Company, 1953). There are a number of intermediate economic texts in the field of national income theory. Among the more useful are: Martin Bailey, *National Income and the Price Level* (New York: McGraw-Hill Book Company, 1962); Barry Siegel, *Aggregate Economics and Public Policy* (Homewood, Ill.: Richard D. Irwin, Inc., 1960); and Gerald Sirkin, *Introduction to Macro-economic Theory* (Homewood, Ill.: Richard D. Irwin, Inc., 1961). The application of national income theory to the problem of economic fluctuations is handled in a very compact way by R. C. O. Matthews, *The Business Cycle* (Chicago: University of Chicago Press, 1959), especially Chapters I–VII. Gardner Ackley's *Macroeconomic Theory* (New York: The Macmillan Company, 1961) is a comprehensive, lucid, advanced treatment.

A discussion of the various kinds of inflation and their characteristics is contained in C. L. Schultze, *Recent Inflation in the United States* (Study Paper No. 1, U.S. Congress, Joint Economic Committee, *Study of Employ-*

*ment, Growth and Price Levels, 1959*; see Chapter 1 for a summary analysis). *The Wage–Price Issue* by William Bowen (Princeton, N.J.: Princeton University Press, 1960) discusses the dilemma posed for public policy by "spontaneous" increases in costs and prices.

In *Economic Development: Past and Present*, 2nd ed., Foundations of Modern Economics (Englewood Cliffs, N.J.: Prentice-Hall, Inc., 1967), Richard Gill provides an introduction to the theory of economy growth. Chapters 1–4 discuss growth from the viewpoint of the advanced industrial countries. In *Economic Growth, An American Problem* (Englewood Cliffs, N.J.: Prentice-Hall, Inc., 1964), Peter Gutmann has brought together a series of essays by different authors on the subject of economic growth in the United States. This volume presents several different views on each of the major problems associated with economic growth. A similar volume, edited by Edmund Phelps, is *The Goal of Economic Growth* (New York: W. W. Norton & Company, Inc., 1962). Edward Denison's *The Sources of Economic Growth in the United States* (Committee for Economic Development, Supplementary Paper No. 13, 1962) attempts to determine the relative importance of the various factors which have contributed to economic growth.

Good summaries of the basic facts about American economic growth are found in the testimony of Raymond Goldsmith and Solomon Fabricant before the Joint Economic Committee (*Study of Employment, Growth and Price Levels*, Hearings, Part II, 1959). Professor Simon Kuznets, a pioneer in the field of measuring national income, compares various aspects of the economic growth of the industrial countries of the world in *Six Lectures on Economic Growth* (New York: The Free Press, 1960).

The *Staff Report* of the Joint Economic Committee's *Study of Employment Growth and Price Levels* (1960) is a good example of the application of many aspects of aggregate economic theory to various problems of public policy. Similar examples may be found in the annual *Economic Report of the President*. The January 1962 *Economic Report* is a particularly good case in point. Another excellent sample of applied national income theory is Bert Hickman's *Growth and Stability of the Postwar Economy* (Washington, D.C.: The Brookings Institution, 1960), especially Part III. An outstanding example for another country is J. C. R. Dow, *The Management of the British Economy, 1945–60* (Cambridge, England: Cambridge University Press, 1964).

# Index